MY LIFE, MY CHOICES

Key Issues for Young Adults

by Mary Ann Burkley Wojno

*To Susie
With love and best wishes,
Mary Ann Burkley Wojno*

Paulist Press
New York/Mahwah, N.J.

The Publisher gratefully acknowledges use of the following materials: excerpts quoted in Christopher News Note 347, *The Power of Forgiveness*, and used with permission of The Christophers, 12 East 48th Street, New York, NY; reprint of "B.C.," by Johnny Hart, used by permission of Johnny Hart and Creators Syndicate, Inc.; reprint of "For Better or For Worse" © 1994 Lynn Johnston Prod., Inc. Reprinted with permission of Universal Press Syndicate. All rights reserved. Quotations by Rosemary Brown from, *No Way!, Not Me,* The National Film Board of Canada, 1251 Avenue of the Americas, 16th Floor, New York, NY 10020; excerpts from *The Greatest Salesman in the World,* by Lifetime Books, Hollywood, CA (800-771-3355), copyright © by Og Mandino. Reprinted with permission. Reprint of *The Social Readjustment Scale,* from *The Journal of Psychosomatic Research*; reprinted by permission of the publisher from *The Journal of Psychosomatic Research,* Vol. II, #2, pp. 213-218, copyright © 1967, by Elsevier Science, Inc., 655 Avenue of the Americas, New York, NY 10010. Excerpts from "Student Stress: Why You're Uptight and What to Do About It," published in SIGN magazine, The Passionist Fathers, Union City, NJ 07087. Excerpts from *The Greatest Miracle in the World,* by Lifetime Books, Hollywood, CA (800-771-3355), copyright © by Og Mandino. Reprinted with permission.

Cover by Cindy Dunne

Book design by Céline M. Allen

Copyright © 1997 by Mary Ann Burkley Wojno

All rights reserved. No part of this book may be reproduced or transmitted in any form or by any means, electronic or mechanical, including photocopying, recording or by any information storage and retrieval system without permission in writing from the Publisher.

ISBN: 0-8091-3682-1

Published by Paulist Press
997 Macarthur Boulevard
Mahwah, New Jersey 07430

Printed and bound in the United States of America

CONTENTS

Introduction — v

1. In Search of Self — 1
   - Here I Am   1
   - Identity Sheet   4
   - Plus and Minus IDs   7

2. My Silent Self — 11
   - My Silent Self   11
   - My One Physical Aspect I Would Change   15
   - Mental Attitude Toward Self   19
   - Overcoming Handicaps   23

3. Taking Control of My Life — 27
   - Intrinsic Treasures   27
   - A Personal Crest   31
   - What Other People Might Say   33
   - Are You in Control of Your Life?   37

4. Student Stress — 43
   - Student Stress and What to Do About It   44
     - Project Sheet: How Much Stress Have You Experienced?   47
     - Project Sheet: Causes of Stress: A Student Evaluation   48
   - Stress from Worry, Fear, and Rejection   51

5. Generation Gap — 57
   - Who Starts the Arguments at Home? Why?   60
   - Try to Understand Your Parents   65

6. There Is No One To Listen — 71
   - Loneliness for Me   71
   - Loneliness, a Part of Being Human   77

7. Friendship — 81
   - Friendship's Meaning to Me   81
   - Selected Quotations on Friendship   85

8. Peer Pressure — 91
   - Areas of Peer Pressure   91
   - The Harmful Influence of Peer Pressure   95
   - The Harmful Effects of Drugs and Alcohol   101
     - Project Sheet: Know the Law and the Consequences for Using Alcohol   107
     - Project Sheet: Getting Busted for Drugs   108

9. Human Sexuality ... 109
    Focus on Human Sexuality 109
    Human Sexuality: Consider the Consequences 113
        Project Sheet: The Facts about STDs and HIV 119
        Project Sheet: Human Sexuality
                       and the Prospect of Poverty 124
        Project Sheet: Plan Ahead for Your Life 127

10. A Why To Live ... 129
    Suicide 129
    How Can Suicide Be Prevented? 135
    A Why To Live 141

11. A Word Can Mean So Much ... 145
    The Power of *Please* and *Thank You* 145
    Three Little Words: I Love You 149
    Two Big Words: I'm Sorry 153

12. Giving and Receiving ... 159
    Giving and Receiving 159
    What Do You Do With a Compliment? 163
    What Do Other People Do With Compliments? 167

13. Happiness for Me ... 171
    Happiness Log and Survey 171
    Happiness for Me 175

14. The Joys of Living ... 181
    These Things I Remember 181
    Say Yes to Life 189

15. Success in My Life ... 195
    What Is Success? 195
    The Person I Will Marry 201

16. The Final Sharing ... 207
    The Final Sharing 207

Bibliography ... 213

INTRODUCTION

> To live...is to love...and to be loved.
> To die...is to be born again—
> through Him, love eternal.
> By all that we are,
> in all that we give of ourselves,
> to all whom we know,
> we approach death—
> Love Eternal.

To build a philosophy of life, a person must answer for oneself three questions: Who am I? What is life? What is death?

Why This Book?

Welcome to *My Life, My Choices*. As a high school teacher I have often wondered about the loneliness as well as the hopes and pride in the hearts of my students, feelings that might go unheard and that, if spoken, might echo in others and awaken in them the courage to share *their* feelings as to how they looked at themselves, at others, at life. There is surely a great need for the opportunity to release within such young adults the excitement aroused by sharing the thoughts and feelings stored in heart as well as mind.

Thus came into being an elective course at St. Vincent/St. Mary High School in Akron, Ohio. It was designed so that learning was not measured by tests and examinations, but by discussions of important life topics openly shared and/or written in a personal journal. The power and beauty of thoughts shared deeply influence the heart and mind of young people as they search to discover the *who* of their person and to develop a healthy perspective for happiness in life. Thus this program approaches from a student's viewpoint many things that are important to students but about which few people are willing to talk openly. This includes such issues as loneliness, stress, peer pressure, friendship, happiness, success, human sexuality, and suicide.

This short program is designed for use either in schools or in home groups, especially for high-school-age students. It can be done over a single semester, or, if part of a youth group program outside of the school courses, stretched over as many sessions or weeks as deemed useful. Some discussions may prove valuable enough to carry them over to a following session or class, so some flexibility in the number of meetings planned for the completion of the book is desirable.

Objectives of the Program

Before starting, it is important to know where we are going, as well as what we can expect and what we should not expect from our conversation and journal-keeping. Read the following list and think of how these goals concern your own self-growth and development. The exercises in this book are designed to help each participant to:

1) get to know himself or herself better;
2) learn to communicate feelings and concerns about how one looks at oneself, others, and one's life ahead;
3) define positive ways to improve one's self-image;
4) discuss the causes of stress and ways to cope with it;
5) discuss with peers key issues that trouble all young adults, such as loneliness, suicide, peer pressure, sexuality, etc.;
6) realize that the choices made on a daily basis determine the "who" of one's person and the direction of one's life;
7) consider an attitude toward life that is filled with hope and joy;
8) plan ahead for one's life.

Preparing the Sessions

Since this is not intended to be a formal classroom course, the setting should be as informal and casual as possible. Participants should sit in a circle so that each might be able to look into the faces of the others. A comfortable room such as a lounge would be ideal, but if a more traditional classroom is used, it should—as much as possible—be treated as though it were not a classroom. Participants may prefer to sit on a carpeted floor or lean against a wall. In any case, the atmosphere should from the start be non-threatening and welcoming so that all feel free to contribute to the discussion and are encouraged to do so without risk of judgment or grades.

Establish at the beginning that this is a discussion course or program, and that there will be no quizzes or exams. However, each student is responsible for keeping a journal as part of every session. If this is a regular elective course in school, then whatever grading is needed can be based on students' journal entries, willing participation in the discussions, and a final sharing at the end. Each student should get for himself or herself a journal book in which to write reflections and responses to questions at each of the sessions.

The Structure of the Individual Chapters (Sessions)

The Table of Contents lists the major issues or topics for discussion at each session, and the order in which they will be treated. Each session focuses on a single topic, and the sessions are structured around the Exercise/Journal Sheets. A foreword or short introduction addressed to the topic is followed by the group discussion and then time for entries into the journal.

a) *Reading the introductory passage.* After welcoming the group to the session and putting everyone at ease, the leader should announce the topic. Participants then take turns reading the preliminary remarks. These readings, which precede each journal exercise, establish a basis for the discussion of the topic. Before inviting discussion, any pertinent questions about the reading should be answered. During this period, all are welcomed to note remarks or list ideas in their journals.

b) *The discussion.* A student reader should take the four to six questions on each of the Exercise/Journal Sheets one at a time and allow time for the discussion of each question in turn. It is suggested that an agreed order of rotation be followed. The leader might begin by asking for a volunteer to read and comment on the first question, and then move around the circle from left to right until all have had an opportunity to offer a comment. This ensures that each has the opportunity to participate and respond, and yet does not pressure anyone for a carefully thought out and prepared presentation. An alternative is to have the person who reads the introductory remark also clearly read aloud the questions one by one. The leader can then invite the members to give their comments and recognize each person as he or she indicates readiness. Other arrangements can be decided upon, but whatever order is chosen should also leave room for spontaneous and peripheral additional remarks from others in the group. Provision should be made for a student to pass, and perhaps contribute at a later time.

If the discussion of the questions is intense, and the time for the session is becoming short, it may be possible to carry over the discussion to the next session.

c) *Writing the essay.* At the bottom of each Exercise/Journal Sheet is an essay assignment. The participant may choose a topic from the discussion questions, or may choose a quote from the opening reading, noting the page number. Each person should write in his or her journal a reflection on the question or topic, which will include these three steps:

1) relating the issue to yourself or to someone you know well;

2) citing one or more concrete examples;

3) writing your own reactions (or the other person's, if applicable).

Occasionally someone may prefer to compose a poem or meditation rather than formally addressing the question. This is welcomed, but not as a regular way of avoiding expressing one's own thinking on a topic. Participants may pass in reading their essays aloud to the group, but they should be definitely written down in the journal.

A final word on the structure of the sessions. The leader and group should freely accept what the participant is willing to give. All must be patient with those who are reluctant or slow to participate, or who find it hard to express themselves aloud. For some, listening is very important even if they speak little. All should be attentive to writing their thoughts in their journal, and if a participant has trouble doing even this, the leader can offer simple help and advice on how to put down thoughts in writing. Let the basic rules of the sessions always be kindness, mutual encouragement, and enjoyment in hearing from others.

Acknowledgments

I extend my sincere thanks to Merrylou Windhorst, Suzanne Kozub, and Rev. Thomas Ryan, S.J., for their assistance in gathering journal sheets in some of their classes; to Dr. James Hardy, University of Akron, for his sustained interest in the development of this program; and to Dr. Sara Throop, Youngstown State University, for her guidance and editing of the manuscript.

1   IN SEARCH OF SELF

OBJECTIVES:

1. To get to know myself better
2. To discover the facets of my personality
3. To discover my identity with most positive traits
4. To consider ways to redeem negative identities

Many people spend their lives as trees in a forest. There is no reaching out. They live in the shadow of other people, dwarfed by tradition and convention or confined by prejudice and insecurity, never to know the fullness of themselves or the joy of living.

Youth is fleeting. Yet much of how we live our lives is dependent upon the choices we make in our youth. Good decisions depend upon how well we know ourselves and how well we prepare ourselves for the future.

In searching for ourselves, it is necessary to consider the who of our person—the many aspects of our personality. Each of us has as many facets to his or her life as the limbs and branches of a great tree. Those reaching out develop, leaf, and bloom with ever more branching, ever more blooming, ever more living.

HERE I AM

Personal relationships constitute major branches for possible individual growth. Family identities include son/daughter, sibling, grandson/granddaughter, niece/nephew, in-law, godchild, and step relationships. But each facet of identity must be recognized as important by the individual for the relationship to have a positive or a negative impact on the individual. Interaction within a relationship by an individual determines the strength of that specific identity.

Family relationships have such a great potential for positive individual growth. If a person within a family is nourished with love and caring, that family relationship will form an anchor of security from which to reach out and grow. The family forms the lens through which one first sees life. By the very nature of closeness, though, these same family identities can be the source of pain, fear, and insecurity—negative identities that bind and encumber.

Friend, best friend, boyfriend/girlfriend, acquaintance, neighbor, peer, fellow employee, classmate, club member, teammate—each is an individual identity through which we respond to life in a special way, positive or negative.

Talents, interests, hobbies, and activities—pet owner, driver, politics, religion, race, sex, handicap, age, etc.—add identities in almost unending combinations. Each one is a separate facet constituting the uniqueness of our person.

Actions and reactions to any given facet add color to our personality. The further we develop an identity, the more it will help shape the who of our person.

Our identities can be shown graphically on a pinwheel. To borrow from mathematics, a point is an idea. Let the point be an individual. An infinite number of lines may intersect in a single point. Let each half-line radiating from the point represent an identity determined by personal relationships, talents, avocations, employment, interests, etc. With a little reflection we may find a surprising number of facets, each adding dimension and outlining, in a sense, the myriad aspects of our person.

As we choose to read our list of identities, the class will get a first view into our personality. Our individual interpretations add dimension, and there is the beginning of acquaintance with both ourselves and each other.

STUDENT DISCUSSION

Ned is the first to give a profile of his person. "Son, brother, uncle, cousin, friend, best friend, grandson, great-grandson, gun owner, Republican, cigar smoker, hunter, Catholic, outdoorsman, artist, writer, student, fisherman."

Another young man reads from his pinwheel. "Student, employee, skier, tennis player, football player, goalie, pet owner, boyfriend, nephew, Irishman, Scot, humorist, listener, dreamer, sports fan, neighbor, artist, male, son, brother, teammate, best friend, grandson, cousin."

Oral disclosures are very meaningful. A young woman names her identities as: "Daughter, stepdaughter, sister, stepsister, granddaughter, friend, cousin, neighbor, best friend, senior, U.S. citizen, employee, co-worker, godchild, coach, counselor, statistic, social security number, National Honor Society member, reader, volleyball player, eighteen years old, female, acquaintance, Christian."

Another young woman gives her identity a broader focus. She lists important events in her life corresponding to age level. "... First grade: I admired my sister, could write cursive, met my best friend.... Eighth grade: May crowning court, confirmation, high school scholarship. ... 12th grade: 3.5 grade point, part-time job, active social life, conflict with my mom, register to vote, decisions on college/career. I am a young black woman who plans to achieve as far as my potential will take me."

Objectives: *To get to know myself better*
To discover the facets of my personality

EXERCISE/JOURNAL SHEET

HERE I AM

Facets of my life. A point is an idea. Let the point be you. Let each line represent a facet of your life—an identity. Name each line with a relationship (son/daughter, athlete, etc.). Add lines as you need them.

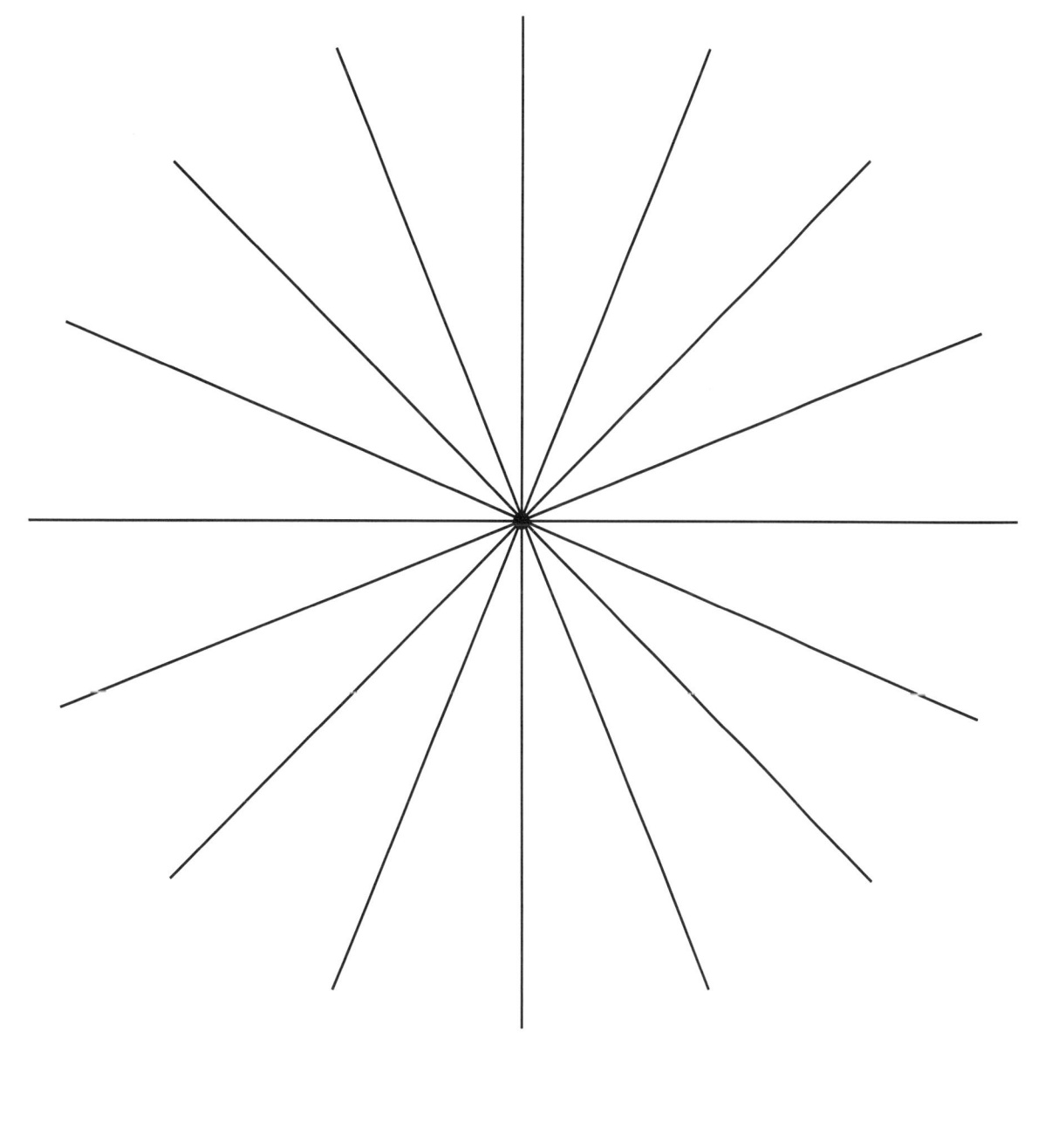

IDENTITY SHEET

How well do we know ourselves? Imagine defining the who of our person in terms of personality traits. Consider the effect of environment on the way we act or react. There are people with whom and circumstances in which we may be very outgoing. On the contrary, we may feel restrained and inhibited with other people and/or in a different environment. We react differently within each identity as we respond to our environment at a given point in our life.

We gain an insight into our real selves by making split-second decisions as to which facet of our personality reflects best self, most confident, most competitive, most worried, etc. By evaluating each trait as positive (+) or negative (-), an even greater understanding of a given relationship is obtained.

Listening to disclosures made by our peers, we are often surprised by a person's response to a given identity. We learn firsthand that as individuals we look at ourselves and at life differently. This is as it should be. Many of us have never thought about how we act or react in terms of mood at home versus mood with friends or at school.

By sharing honest comments, we realize how much we have in common with others. Each honest comment inspires truthful admissions from others, and dialogue may begin.

STUDENT DISCUSSION/ESSAY

Replies to the matching of a personality trait with an identity is provocative. Consider:

Best self: friend, best friend, home, school.

Most aggressive: athlete, debater, brother/sister, employee.

Identity (ID) with most worries: college/job, myself, future, school, friend, student, friends in school.

Most pressure: student, friend, college applicant, daughter/son, athlete, employee, job choice.

Some students acknowledge being *most competitive* at home, with themselves, or as siblings, while others mention soccer, wrestling, or football.

For *most conflict* many cite mom, dad, sister, brother, daughter, and student.

Some young women cite friend as the identity where they did the *most talking* and *most listening*.

Athlete is identified as *hardest to achieve, most criticism,* and *most praise.*

Objective: *To get to know myself better*   EXERCISE/JOURNAL SHEET

IDENTITY SHEET

Match each of the following traits with the identity that first comes to mind. Make split-second decisions. To the left of each number indicate the trait as (+) positive or (-) negative.

__ 1. Best self _____   __ 18. Most moody _____

__ 2. Most aggressive _____   __ 19. Best ego _____

__ 3. Most friendly _____   __ 20. Hardest to achieve _____

__ 4. Most unfriendly _____   __ 21. Someone only a few know _____

__ 5. Most at peace _____   __ 22. Most trusted _____

__ 6. Most expected of you _____   __ 23. Most competitive _____

__ 7. Most rewarding _____   __ 24. Taken for granted _____

__ 8. Most secure _____   __ 25. Most criticism _____

__ 9. Give the most _____   __ 26. Most praise _____

__ 10. Most open, natural _____   __ 27. Most respected _____

__ 11. Most disliked ID _____   __ 28. Most influential _____

__ 12. Most pressure _____   __ 29. A confidant(e) _____

__ 13. ID like to discard _____   __ 30. Most talkative _____

__ 14. ID like best _____   __ 31. Most willing to listen _____

__ 15. Most appreciated _____   __ 32. Most worries _____

__ 16. Most understood _____   __ 33. Greatest hopes _____

__ 17. Requires understanding _____   __ 34. Greatest fears _____

WRITE A SHORT ESSAY on the mood that most often refers to you. Cite an example.

TOPIC: _____ DATE: _____

Quote from Reading (pp._____) _____

PLUS AND MINUS IDs

An accounting of the (+) and (-) personality traits as designated on the Identity Sheet are used to describe the identity assigned to it. Once they are listed, it is easy to determine which identity receives the most positive traits, as well as the identity receiving the most negative traits. Sometimes the analysis is surprising.

We react differently within each identity responding to our own environment, at a given point in our lives. Many teenagers list son/daughter as a negative identity. They find their parents demanding of their time and critical of their behavior. However, often a few years later as young married people with families, their parents, with their love and caring, will reflect for them the most positive relationship.

It is also true that an important identity in our lives may have many negative traits. For example, a mother might respond with many negative characteristics regarding her station in life—most criticism, most expected of her, most taken for granted. Under the ID labeled *most like to discard,* the tasks of cleaning lady and ironing lady might be an honest admission, and yet motherhood is perhaps her most cherished identity.

The identities that have the most influence on our lives can be easily recognized by the traits ascribed to the specific identities in this exercise. People who have set definite goals may wish to consider if their current personal relationships are leading them in the direction of their choice.

A person desiring to take control of his or her life might consider ways of redeeming negative ID(s). Since the identity is recognized as important in the individual's life, it may be a worthwhile challenge to reflect on efforts that will turn that identity around— to be the best one can be.

The positive actions a person can take can be as simple as sharing a smile and a warm greeting, paying a compliment, saying I love you or saying I'm sorry, doing a favor, or including another in an activity. When we reach out to others and learn to like them, we invariably learn to like ourselves better, too.

STUDENT DISCUSSION/ESSAY

Monica volunteered to open the discussion. "The facet of my personality that receives the most positive traits is friend. The positive traits that I assign to friend are best self, most fun, most at peace, most praise, most open and natural, most trusted, most friendly, most listening, and greatest hope. My identity receiving the most negative traits is sister. The traits I assign to this identity are most worry, most pressure, most criticism, most aggressive, most moody. I would like to be closer to my sister. I think that eventually I will, after I move out and get some space. The positive action I could take would be go out of my way and try to do nice things for her."

Julie raised her hand. "My list of negative traits would have paralleled yours a year ago, Monica. My sister is younger than I am, and she claims that all of the good things happen to me first. I never thought much about her remark until one morning at breakfast when I told her that she looked nice. I couldn't believe what she did. She marched up to her room and changed her outfit! I was overwhelmed that I had so alienated her. Since then I have found ways to regain her confidence and love. My first approach was to make time for her."

In an essay assignment a young man wrote, "I have never thought about how I act and react with my friends as being different than the way I act at home. Then I remembered something my mother used to say about me and my brother when we were in grade school. She called us 'street angels and house devils.' We often argued in the morning as we got ready for school. My mother would send us outside to wait for the bus, fighting, but as soon as other children came to wait with us, we were all smiles."

Objectives: *To discover my identity that has the most positive traits*
To consider ways to reinforce negative identities

Exercise/Journal Sheet

PLUS AND MINUS IDs

1. My identity receiving the most positive traits is _____.

   The positive traits credited to this identity are:

2. My identity receiving the most negative traits is _____

   The negative traits credited to this identity are:

3. What positive action can be taken in little ways to turn around a negative identity? Cite an example.

4. In nurturing a negative relationship, do you think that you might like yourself better? Why?/Why not?

WRITE A SHORT ESSAY on one of the topics or CHOOSE A QUOTE from the readings. Relate it to yourself or someone you know. Cite an example. Include reactions—yours and theirs.

TOPIC: _____ DATE: _____

Quote from Reading (pp._____) _____

2 MY SILENT SELF

OBJECTIVES:

1. To share how I look at myself, others, and life
2. To discuss areas of personal insecurity
3. To elicit ways of overcoming perceived handicaps

"If people knew me as I really am, they would love me for being human like them." David Richo, in his book *How To Be an Adult,* uses these words to define a healthy adult. Why is it then that we fear letting others get to know us? Why do we hold in our silent selves the human clues to who we are?

MY SILENT SELF

We know ourselves only as others see us. For this reason we desire to share what we see, what we think, and what we feel with someone whom we know and trust. It is human to want someone as a sounding board for ideas that first come into our view—to say things aloud and to get the feedback that sharing provides. This is a growing experience into adulthood.

To achieve adulthood we must not only come to know ourselves but we must accept who we are, and then take the risk of reaching out and proclaiming it to others. It is our humanity with all of its faults and shortcomings that is as much a part of our person as the facets of our personality. When we can claim ourselves, we can be open to share with others. It is then that the fruits of life can be enjoyed as they are shared. Richo stresses that the starting point of our love for others is our sane and fearless love of ourselves.

As we make disclosures about ourselves we open up new vistas of our person to others, and provide the dynamics for good communication. Sharing the lighter side of ourselves, or touching on general information, is a good beginning for getting to know others.

We are often reticent to give insights into our silent selves, our deep emotion, our inner thoughts. Sometimes we remain silent about ourselves because we think others might interpret what we say as bragging. Why does it seem easier to share disappointments or failure than to share joy or success? Does this fact have to do with us or to the reaction of those with whom we share?

In our insecurity, we may hide our real feelings because others might be critical, judgmental, or prejudiced.

Sometimes our sharing holds a different meaning—that of looking at an event in our lives and remembering the hurt. Getting a thought out into the open often can dilute the disappointment and permit its being taken back and accepted.

Our disclosures about ourselves or our families form gut level communication that speaks of our sensitivity and pride, our worry of rejection. These sincere admissions often act as a starting point for conversations and bring about the admiration that comes from mutual insight.

STUDENT DISCUSSION/ESSAY

"I'm quiet and shy at school, but loud at home. I have a sense of humor. I have two sisters. I want to have a career, and I hope to have a large family." Toni was first to speak.

A young man was very brief. He said, "I'm quiet, conservative, nice, open with a friend, willing to help."

A second young man was also brief. "I like to write. I like to build and create things. I'm interested in politics. I read books on business art."

Marcy spoke next. "I have an extra toe. I have lived in seven states. I have attended eight different schools. I have two brothers and a sister. I can bend my thumb back to my wrist." She grinned as she finished, and showed her flexible thumb trick. No one else could do it.

A sensitive young man placed his books on the floor beside him as he joined the circle of participants. He seemed to light up as he volunteered to share something of his silent self. "I crawl out of my bedroom window and sit on the garage roof on a summer night. It's my private space. I dream of riding across the country on my bike. Someday, I will."

Then a tall, willowy girl stated, "Few people know that I won second place in the National Fred Astaire Dance Contest." Her amazed classmates blurted out: "Really! When? How?" Almost timidly, she continued, "I'm the youngest in my family. Both of my parents work. It was my oldest sister's responsibility to care for me after school. My sister was a dance instructor at the local Fred Astaire Dance Studio. She would take me along. As a youngster, I watched from the sidelines, and mimicked the routines. Ballroom dancing was so much a part of my early years that it became second nature to me. By the time I entered high school, I, too, was a dance instructor. A ballerina-length dress and an upswing hairstyle added sophistication to my years. Last year the national dance competition was held in Florida. It was an all-expense-paid trip. My sister went with me. This time she was on the sidelines."

Some admissions from the students' private lives were more poignant than exciting. Mary, a bright, conscientious student had a feeling of pride to share. "My grandparents came from Russia," she said, in her quiet way. "Grandfather came first. It took him seven years to save up enough money to go back and get his bride. I often think about the love they shared that could wait so long apart."

A girl with high cheekbones and black hair that was pulled back into a bun shook her head despondently as she told of a broken dream. "I have studied ballet since childhood. It had become a part of my life and that of my parents. We had so many plans. Yes, I aspired to be a ballerina." Her eyes dropped as she confessed, "When I talked to my instructor about my future in dance, he said, quite pointedly, that I lacked the physical makeup to qualify for further study."

Hearing the admissions of others often opens the floodgates that bring about acceptance of ourselves or our family. "My dad's an alcoholic. He makes things difficult at home," admitted a young woman. "But I tell my friends: if you are my friend, you will come over to my house and not pay him any mind. Remember you are coming to see me."

For her final sharing at the semester's end, a quiet, poised, young woman told of learning to love her mother. This gentle student, who had listened for many days, shared an event so heartfelt that she touched every student's life with her maturity, her pride, and her joy. "My mother," she began, "was constantly badgering me about my hair, my clothes, my friends. Then one day last summer Mom had a heart attack, and I was left in charge at home while she was in the hospital. There was so much to be done. It was so quiet around the table at dinner with her chair empty. My dad was so sad.... She improved. When she was coming home, they said that I had to take care of her. I'm not a nurse. I didn't want to do this. But I couldn't say no. I couldn't admit how I felt. Then as I did little things for her, she seemed to change. She was so grateful for the smallest kindness. My father was so happy. By the time school started, Mom was back in charge again. It was during those days that I learned to love my mom and I learned that she loved me, too."

Objective: To communicate my feelings on how
I look at myself, at others, and at life

EXERCISE/JOURNAL SHEET

MY SILENT SELF

1. List five things that few people know about you:

   a.

   b.

   c.

   d.

   e.

2. Comment on each of the following as they pertain to the fact that sometimes you hesitate to disclose your feelings about your real self because

   a. others might interpret what you say as bragging

   b. others might be critical or judgmental

   c. others might be prejudiced

3. Does it seem easier to share disappointments or failure than to share joy or success? Why? With whom?

WRITE A SHORT ESSAY on one of the topics or CHOOSE A QUOTE from the readings. Relate it to yourself or to someone you know. Cite an example. Include the effect on you, on others.

TOPIC: _____ DATE: _____

Quote from Reading (pp._____) _____

MY ONE PHYSICAL ASPECT I WOULD CHANGE

We often rationalize a personal shortcoming as being something over which we have no control. Each of us can name at least one physical aspect of our person that we would like to change, because we perceive its effect as a cause for insecurity in our life.

Within our silent self, we often think that if we could just change our nose or our ears, or whatever, life would be fuller, success easier, and friendships more readily achieved. We tend to think that we see ourselves as others see us, but is this true? We are surprised when a peer with naturally curly hair wishes her hair were straight, or a thin girl wishes that she could put on weight.

In today's world, marketing caters to the popular desire to reflect the TV image: long eyelashes, tapered fingernails, a slim feminine figure—or a trim, robust, male physique. Beauty salons, spas, exercise clinics make it possible for us to fulfill many of our desires for physical change, and thus achieve the look we desire for our best self.

Today, there are so many things we can do to accomplish that look we desire, including the right clothes. However, to be truly satisfied with ourselves, we must find happiness within and with ourselves.

STUDENT DISCUSSION/ESSAY

Ken, a football player, who was team co-captain with All-City recognition, opened the discussion. He said, "Just two more inches and twenty more pounds, and I could have had a college scholarship." He paused and then added, "But I'm a much nicer person today than I was as a football player."

"I always wanted red hair and green eyes, so I dye my hair and wear tinted contacts!" admitted a feisty young woman. Laughter followed her admission. "My brother always tells people that he is 5′ 7″. One day I caught him saying it. He laughed and admitted that he is only 5′ 6″ tall, but said that it made him feel better about himself to say 5′ 7″!" The memory made her smile.

Four years after high school graduation, a slightly built young man surprised his former classmates by being named "Mr. Ohio" in winning the men's body-building contest. He did something about attaining the personal image that he had held for himself.

Annalisa told of a family friend who did her medical internship in plastic surgery, but switched to obstetrics. "She told us that cosmetic surgery can give people the facial features they choose, but that the surgeons can't change the way the people feel about themselves. She said that during a summer experience on a reservation, she shared such joy with some Indian women in the birth of their babies that she chose ob-gyn as her field for further study."

One young woman spoke of craving independence. She got a part-time job at a department store, and shortly thereafter opened her own charge account. Some time later, she opened a bank checking account. She did something about her desire for independence. She began to create it.

Objective: To discuss insecurity as perceived in physical handicaps EXERCISE/JOURNAL SHEET

MY ONE PHYSICAL ASPECT I WOULD CHANGE

Have you ever rationalized a physical shortcoming as being something over which you have no control? If you have ever felt this way, what would you change, and how do you perceive the change would affect your life?

1. What would you change, and how?

2. What effect do you think the change would have on your life?

3. What physical aspects of your person have you changed (contacts, nails, fitness, etc.)? Explain.

4. Have these changes made a difference in the way that you feel about yourself? Explain.

5. Are you making a deliberate effort to become the person that you want to be?

WRITE A SHORT ESSAY from the topics above or CHOOSE A QUOTE from the readings. Relate it to self/others. Cite an example. Include the effect on you, and the effect you perceived it to have on others.

TOPIC: _____ DATE: _____

Quote from Reading (pp._____) _____

MENTAL ATTITUDE TOWARD SELF

People who love themselves love others, and love life. Love is an enabler. Love is an energizer. To love is to live. But how many of us really accept ourselves, and love ourselves? How many of us awaken happy in the morning, and are anxious for the challenges of a new day? We have so many advantages that we often overlook—good health, energy, stamina, and the opportunities to determine who and what we want to be.

Besides the physical aspects of our person that we would change, there are often other attributes that we may feel keep us from being our best. Our mental attitude—how we look at ourselves, and the way we look at life—can create a negative response known as depression, or the positive response of a happy person. We need to recognize our mental attitude, and see its reflection in how we look at life.

When our words speak of a poor self-image and a negative outlook on life, our mirror of self does not reflect our vast potential of talent, our eagerness of heart, nor our beauty of soul.

STUDENT DISCUSSION/ESSAY

Eric opened the discussion with an admission of his insecurity. "I have low self-confidence, and I am not determined enough about what I want to accomplish with my life."

"I fear rejection. I look to the past and think about what might have been," said another youth.

"I'm insecure. My family has always moved around a lot. I can't stay any place for a long time," a nervous girl conceded. "I can't even accept compliments."

"I worry a lot. I actually worry myself sick," put in another student during this open confession of insecurities.

"I don't like myself. Emotionally, I look at things negatively, including life, and wonder why I should try." These statements were made by a lovely young woman who appeared to have it all together.

"I lack self-confidence. I'm oversensitive. I'm cynical about life and somewhat overweight," admitted a young woman who was struggling to achieve the look she desired, and hadn't accepted the who of her person.

"I make life a competition. I can't accept failure. I have to fit in. I'm a perfectionist." The words were short and clipped from a girl who seemed to be struggling emotionally with herself.

Karen, whose mother was dying of cancer, told of a letter that her mother had written to her from the hospital. "At the end of the letter my mom lists the names of the people who love me, starting with family members. Mom told me to read their names over and over, and to let the thought of their love empower me. I guess Mom doesn't think the memory of her love will be enough."

Objective: To acknowledge perceived emotional handicaps EXERCISE/JOURNAL SHEET

MENTAL ATTITUDE TOWARD SELF

People who love themselves love others, and love life. Think about yourself and comment on the following.

1. Describe the way you feel about yourself.

2. Are you happy with who you are? Why?/Why not?

3. Where do you feel most secure? Why?

4. Make a list of those who love you.

Read your list of those who love you. Read it again. Keep their names in your heart. Let them empower you to become the best you can be. Open your mind. Open your heart. Share your love.

WRITE A SHORT ESSAY from the topics above or CHOOSE A QUOTE from the readings. Relate it to yourself. Cite an example.

TOPIC: _____ DATE: _____

Quote from Reading (pp. _____) _____

OVERCOMING HANDICAPS

Handicaps take many forms: physical, which we must accept; emotional, which is the way we feel about ourselves; and mental, which is the way we look at ourselves and at life. Handicaps cause negative vibes within us—we might feel we're not good enough; or we may use a handicap as a crutch to rationalize the seeming inequities of life. Overcoming a handicap establishes the possibility of changing our lives.

How can we overcome our negative feelings about ourselves and about life? Can we recall a handicap that we have overcome? Did it change our attitude about ourselves and about life? If we prefer, we can share the handicap that someone whom we know and admire overcame.

Overcoming handicaps is the proving ground for people as they are questioned by life. Learning to meet the problems posed on a daily basis with a positive attitude is the growing experience that leads to maturity. No one is exempt from life's anxieties, life's pain, and sorrow. It is how we carry our burdens that determines our measure in life.

STUDENT DISCUSSION/ESSAY

A young man was the first to speak in this discussion. "My anxieties about school were so acute that my parents took me to a psychologist who taught me self-hypnosis. Now when I get uptight before a test or a new situation, I can relax myself. It has helped me."

"I've always been shy," admitted a smiling coed. "When I came to high school, I decided to be a new me. I did it by being more open, being the first to say hello, and by volunteering to help."

"My mother worked, and my grandmother lived with us. Grandma died two days before my First Communion," acknowledged a very sincere young teen. "It took a long time for me to overcome the loss of her presence in my life."

"My aunt had polio. She lived for a time in an iron lung. She was one of eighteen children, and was passed around to foster families. She became all that they said she could never achieve. Today, she is married, has a child, and has earned her master's degree in business. If she can do all of that, then I'm encouraged to see what I can do with my life." Joe was proud to share this memory.

A young woman brought in a copy of a "B.C." comic strip (Hart, 1988). "I brought in this comic to share with you an example of courage that I have witnessed in my family. My great aunt, at the age of 89, had a leg amputated above the knee. She continues to live alone in her apartment in Manhattan. This comic was on her Christmas card a year after her surgery. Read it. It speaks of her positive attitude."

B.C. by Johnny Hart

Lynne signaled to speak next. "I am blind in my right eye, and farsighted in my left eye. I have had seven eye surgeries to try to correct the problem. The doctors say that I am unable to have any more. I have been told that I have a 50/50 chance of losing my sight altogether, or have it remain the same. I want to go to law school, so I hope my eyesight will last until then. While in college, I plan to learn Braille so I will be able to go on with my career. I have learned to accept the possibility of going blind, and I am grateful that I have been given this much time, so far."

No one had realized her physical handicap. Her acceptance, positive attitude, and plan for her life were her means of coping.

Anne followed Lynne in speaking. "I have asthma. I developed it as a teenager, and now it is pretty serious. I think of it as a handicap, because sometimes it prevents me from doing things with my friends. It also prevents me from participating in athletics, because simply by running, my lungs become tight and breathing becomes difficult. To compensate for this, I have become very active in extracurricular activities. I have just redirected my goals to use the talents I have effectively."

Bridgette spoke of a different kind of handicap. "I was afraid to lean on others, because I could not trust people. I had trouble being open with others, thinking they would make fun of me. I always did everything for myself. I wanted no help because to me it symbolized weakness. I remained strong even when I was deeply upset, to show others that nothing affected me. In recent years, through close relationships with friends, I have learned to open up to others and to express my views and feelings. It has helped me to be a happier person, and I am able to face difficult situations."

For her final sharing, Michelle told of her experience as a camp counselor. She read from an essay that she had sent with her application to the University of Notre Dame. "I chose to share this, because it tells of my answer to the question of overcoming a handicap, and of releasing myself to an eagerness to reach out to life.

"I was so nervous in driving to the camp. I didn't really want to go, and I had an overwhelming desire to turn around and go home. I was lonely, already, just with the thought of this new experience. But I drove on. Deep down I knew that I had so much to prove to myself and to my family.

"The first week was so hard. I hated the training. I hated being a newcomer. I just wanted to forget it all, and go home. But I stayed. Then I found that as I accepted, I was accepted. As I overcame, I became an adult. I found that I was respected for my own being. I gained self-confidence and with it came responsibility. I even won over a young girl's fears with love and kindness. I never worked so hard for such low pay before in my life, and yet I was most fully rewarded, because I had developed the independence and maturity that I needed to go to college." She was accepted at Notre Dame!

Objective: To find ways of overcoming handicaps   Exercise/Journal Sheet

OVERCOMING HANDICAPS

Handicaps take many forms: physical, which we must accept; emotional, which is the way we feel about ourselves; and mental, which is the way we look at ourselves and at life.

Comment on each of the following types of handicaps as they pertain(ed) to you.

1. Physical handicap:

2. Emotional handicap:

3. Mental handicap:

4. Have you or would you want to overcome one or more of your handicaps?

5. Has overcoming a handicap changed your attitude about yourself and about life?

6. Have you known someone who overcame a handicap? Explain.

WRITE A SHORT ESSAY on one of the topics or CHOOSE A QUOTE from the readings. Relate it to yourself/someone you know. Cite an example. Include the effect on you.

TOPIC: _____ DATE: _____

Quote from Reading (pp._____) _____

3   TAKING CONTROL OF MY LIFE

OBJECTIVES:

1. To consider intrinsic treasures—personal, family
2. To design a personal crest
3. To consider the impact of other people on my life
4. To question if I am satisfied with who I am
5. To define positive ways to improve my self-image

> Would that I could tell you the things that you quest.
> Would that I could know which way is the best.
> But I am no more than any human—
> Seeking, searching for Divinity's plan,
> Which will lift us up close to Him one day,
> To the great glories that pattern His way.
> Alone I can tell the sensitive heart
> That truth lies within—intrinsic's impart,
> And the vision of good sees with the mind.
> The cherished answers you quest, you shall find,
> If you will seek out what is dearest to you,
> There shall you find what is precious and true.

INTRINSIC TREASURES

Deep within each of us is the knowledge of our own intrinsic treasures that form the core of our person. *Intrinsic* is defined as belonging to the real nature of a thing. What are things, intrinsic, that belong to our own real selves? We might start by saying that they are treasures that cannot be bought or sold, touched or tasted. Intrinsic treasures are seen, when people notice; they are felt, when others show they care. The governing forces of our lives are these treasures of the heart, the interests we plan to pursue, and the goals we hope to attain.

The things that are most important to us will govern and direct our lives. But how many people ever take time to think about what is important to them? Many let their lives be governed by what others want or choose. Some people have no definite plans for their lives, no sense of achievement, other than a mundane daily schedule, and the pleasure of the moment. Not making a choice is a choice.

STUDENT DISCUSSION/ESSAY

Larry is the first to respond in the discussion. "Life, liberty, and the pursuit of happiness are important to me." There was jeering. Larry looked over his peers quickly to see where the sounds came from, and then continued. "I'm serious. I would stand up and be counted for each of these. Interests? I have a lot of different interests, but none that I plan, at least now, to pursue. Life goals? I haven't really thought much about goals, except to be successful at whatever I do."

Linda spoke next. "My family and friends are most important to me. I believe in God and in family values. I would stand up for my family and my friends. I am not sure what interests I might pursue at this point. But I do have a goal for my life. I want somebody to love, a home and a family."

"Money is important to me!" Mike blurted out. "If I have enough money, I can buy whatever I want!"

"Get serious, Mike. The topic is intrinsic treasures." Maggi elbowed him as she spoke. "I know what's important to me: my family, my friends and my faith. I believe in right-to-life, feeding the hungry, and justice for all. I'm interested in art and design. I plan to go to college and major in art."

Jim signaled to speak. "My family values the out-of-doors. They're big on family, too. My dad and uncles take my brother Joe and me hunting in the spring and fishing in the summer. Uncle Dick has a cabin in the mountains. I've learned to appreciate nature, even learned to cook."

"My parents have insisted that college is a must. I've never thought of it in any other way. Their other must is 'save and have,' which is my dad's motto. My mom says that we're thrifty. I'd add good humored and fun." Keith would not be outdone.

Objective: To consider things tangible and intangible that are valued by the person and/or family

EXERCISE/JOURNAL SHEET

INTRINSIC TREASURES

Tangible		*Intangible*	
family	money	faith	trust
friends	hobby	way of life	power
sports	nature	love	humor
talents(s)	music	loyalty	peace
goal	health	honesty	commitment
education	other	integrity	other

Comment on the following:

1. These are most important to me:

2. My family values the following:

3. Beliefs that I would stand up and be counted for:

4. Interests that I have and plan to pursue:

5. Goals that I hope to attain:

WRITE A SHORT ESSAY on one of the topics or CHOOSE A QUOTE from the readings. Relate it to yourself. Cite an example.

TOPIC: _____ DATE: _____

Quote from Reading (pp._____) _____

A PERSONAL CREST

Each of us is aware of those things that are important to us personally. We are aware, as well, of those things that are important to our families. If we put the best of them together with symbols to represent their meaning, we would have the makings of a personal crest.

In early cultures, families prided themselves on their crests. A crest could be the setting of a ring. Letters sealed with a sealing wax bore the imprint of the crest of the sender. Crests were molded of silver, woven into wall hangings, carved out of wood, painted by artisans, and given a place of prominence in the home.

People took time in making their choices of what was important to them, as well as how to symbolize them. Symbols often express meaning better than words.

At the time of the Crusades, a family could be recognized by its coat-of-arms, which symbolized those qualities by which it was known. Crests, coats-of-arms, and/or seals remain in our heritage, notably in our institutions. Consider a school crest, or the federal, state, and local official seals, as well as fraternal organizations to name a few. The symbols on all of these crests represent intrinsic values.

We can achieve the look we desire, and we can determine those intrinsic treasures that give meaning to our lives. But not everyone places the same value on the same things. If we can ascertain personal values for our lives, we have a focus for our lives. This is not to say that our dreams will come true, for fate does play a part in each life. Yet consider a statement from Richard Bach's book *Illusions: The Reluctant Messiah*. He writes that, for every person, all events of his or her life are there because he or she has drawn them there, and what he or she chooses to do with these events is up to him or her.

For most of us, there are always questions: Can I find happiness? Can I know success? Can my goals be attained? The answer to our questions is that we determine our own future on a day-to-day basis, dependent on our choices as life questions us.

We can work toward objectives in the broad sense, but we must deal with life's expectations as well, and often put them in place of our own.

The challenge of symbolizing our values causes us to think of meaning in the simplest terms. Someone asked how one would symbolize the idea of family. A string of stick figures holding hands, or a wreath of hands holding forearms, was suggested.

Objective: To symbolize one's values on a pesonal crest   EXERCISE/JOURNAL SHEET

MY PERSONAL CREST

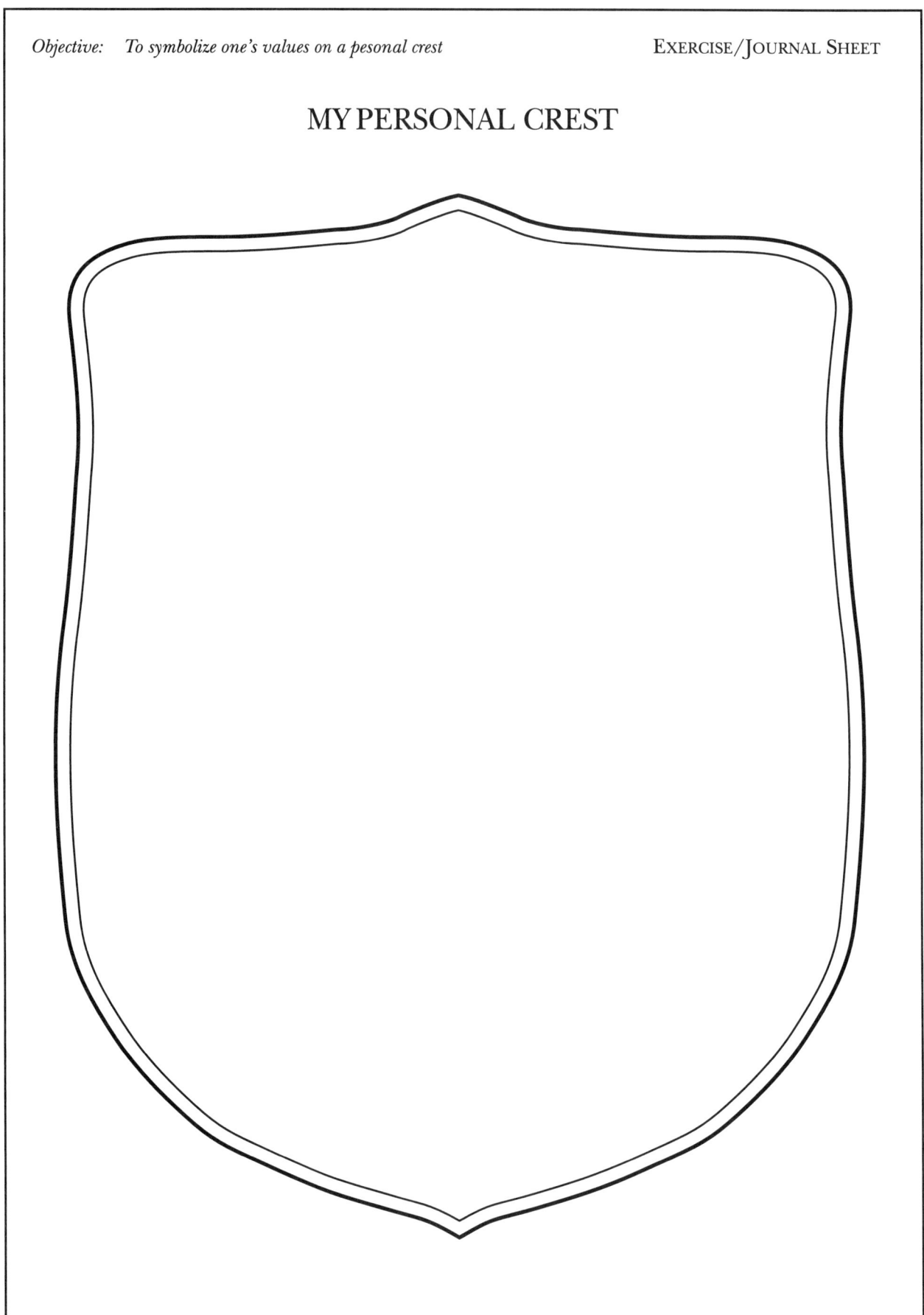

WHAT OTHER PEOPLE MIGHT SAY

We can think of aspects of our lives that few people know about. Generally they are not secrets, but thoughts not spoken in conversation because other people might try to dissuade us, or open us up to criticism. Also when something good happens, there are so few with whom we can share our joy—with whom "my joy is their joy."

In like manner, a seemingly human characteristic is to judge another person's action. So often young people, in particular, worry about taking control of their lives because of what other people might say.

Who are those other people? Do they really care about us or what we do with our lives? Most people are so busy taking care of themselves and their own that their criticism doesn't mean much. When important decisions are to be made about our lives, we should seek mature people whose judgment can be trusted.

Sometimes the other people are those who are close to us. In discussion students revealed that criticism from their parents, siblings, or peers often keeps them from reaching out to try something new.

Sometimes we let the thought of what other people might say keep us a prisoner, with our dreams locked in our hearts. We are afraid to reach out to something new or someone new because we might fail, and this fact keeps us from doing what we would like to do with our lives.

STUDENT DISCUSSION/ESSAY

A young man volunteered to speak first. "I thought about trying out for basketball when I came to high school, but I knew that I couldn't play well enough to please my dad. It was bad enough in junior high. I could hear his voice echoing in the gym. He even conferred with the coach as to my training and his ambitions for me. I disappointed him, and I am sorry about that, but it's my life. I play intramural ball. It's fun and I'm my own person."

"I hear you!" agreed another young man. "I tried out for football, and I made the team. Fortunately, my dad didn't play football. However, there are times when I feel that my life is more his than mine. I'm not interested in playing college football, I want to study art. He just can't understand my position."

Dierdra nodded knowingly, as she spoke. "My brother was promised a career as a pilot when he joined the Air Force. After a month of training, it became clear that even though he was a licensed pilot with a college degree in aviation, he would be trained as a navigator. When he had the opportunity to return to civilian life, he hesitated, because he worried about what other people would say."

"I'm applying to two out-of-state universities," said a very resolute young woman. "They have the best programs in my field. Mom is upset, worrying about the cost. She is sure that I won't get a scholarship. She listens to her bridge club friends, as if they know everything."

"I was going to try out for the musical, but my friends nagged at me. I was sorry I told them," admitted a disappointed teen.

Objective: To consider the impact of other people's comments on how I live my life

EXERCISE/JOURNAL SHEET

WHAT OTHER PEOPLE MIGHT SAY

Have you ever let the thought about what other people might say lock your dreams in your heart? Have you been afraid to reach out, because you might fail?

Comment on each of the questions below. Cite an example. Specify the "other people":

1. In trying out for a team sport?

2. In looking for a special job?

3. In choosing a career?

4. In making a friend?

5. In applying to a particular college?

WRITE A SHORT ESSAY on one of the topics, or CHOOSE A QUOTE from the reading. Relate it to yourself or to someone you know. Cite an example. Include the effect on you and the other person.

TOPIC: _____ DATE: _____

Quote from Reading (pp._____) _____

ARE YOU IN CONTROL OF YOUR LIFE?

Taking control of our life implies taking action toward what we want to become, or what we want to do with our life. As we think about the future, we should focus on the kind of a person we most want to be.

Some people are fortunate in having a role model. Some role models are within one's family, or a friend. They are someone from whose example the person sets his or her own expectations, and from whom to receive encouragement.

Others of us are influenced by people whom we do not know personally, but persons whose charisma and personal feats we have read or heard about which inspire us to be the best we can be.

We are happy when we can accept the who of our person, take charge of our life, and make the most of our time and talents. This is being fully alive.

Life was meant to be enjoyed. When we take control of our life, we become responsible for our choices and our actions.

A good beginning in developing our own person is to determine at least one way—one positive action—that can be taken to improve our self-image in the areas and relationships we feel to be important.

Deciding for ourselves to try something new involves the risk of criticism and the risk of failure. When there is no risk there can be no gain. To be fully alive, we should determine positive actions that we can take in various areas of our life that can improve our image to ourselves as well as others. Each successful action can inspire another, until we become the image of what we want to be. One day, being a positive person can become second nature.

STUDENT DISCUSSION/ESSAY

Academically:

"Do the homework!" This is the one best reply, admitted the majority in the class. Homework done on a daily basis in any given subject will, in time, make students proficient in those disciplines. If questions remain they can be asked in class the following day. Homework done in all subjects every day is the underpinning for academic success.

"Take challenging classes!" Bill called out. The boy who made this suggestion has a goal for his life.

"Pay attention in class; that's what I should do for a start," admitted Ellie, "so I can do my homework."

"I'd have to change where I sit first," joked Larry.

Physically:

"I weight lift as a part of basic athletic training for winter sports," acknowledged Brian.

Student athletes are the exceptions. Students not engaged in team sports came up with a variety of options: jogging or fast walking two miles each day; biking, including group riding on bike trails on weekends; jazzercise, exercise with a TV personality; intramural sports.

"I teach a jazzercise class. I just want to state that the discipline needed to exercise on a regular basis is as important as the exercise itself," Joni announced. "This is true of jogging and other exercises as well."

"Learn a new sport!" put in Nori. "This learning can be fun. Learn to bowl, ski, skate, or play tennis. The best time to learn is when you're a teenager. Then you'll have something to do in your retirement! Like my Granddad."

As a son/daughter:

Teens know in their hearts how to bring joy to a parent and happiness into their home:
"Do what I'm told, when I am told."
"Set the table for dinner without being asked."
"Give my dad a hand when he's fixing the car."
"Be my best self on a daily basis, at home."
"Quit teasing my brothers."

As a brother/sister:

Siblings are eager to give their suggestions.
"Talk to my brother."
"Listen and be patient."
"Make time for them."
"Take my kid brother with me on an errand."
"Go to his ballgames just as he comes to mine."
"Help my sister with her hair. Compliment her."

As a friend:

Serious thought is given to this relationship.
"Be there for them."
"Don't take advantage."
"Include them in what I do."
"Show that I can be trusted."
"Find ways to show that I care about them."
"Return their phone calls."
"Invite them to do something."

As my own person:

Because we know ourselves well, responses come quickly.
"Be on time."
"Quit procrastinating."
"Take an interest in how I look."
"Get a job."
"Save my money."
"Quit smoking."
"Stand up to my peers."
"Take time to smell the flowers."

In the use of my talents:

The list is filled with positive actions.
"First, I have to find mine."
"Set time aside to practice my music."
"Volunteer to do the art work for school events."
"Try out for the school musical."
"Volunteer as a math tutor."
"Turn in a poem to the literary magazine."

In his essay, a young man wrote with pride about his oldest brother's faith in himself and undaunted courage in taking control of his life.
"...I can remember Dad telling my brother that he was wasting his time going out for basketball as a sophomore, because injury had kept him from playing his freshman year. But Bob insisted that playing varsity basketball was something that he wanted to accomplish in high school. He never missed a practice. He followed the suggested individual training. He wanted to learn to jump high, and for this he enlisted me to set the range timer for ten minute intervals, while he practiced jumping rope on the patio. In his junior year he rode the bench, getting in for a few plays each game, but his attitude never changed.

"Three things set him apart: his great height, his love of the game, and his pride in the team. Each time a teammate returned to the bench, Bob stood to greet him, always applauding and usually alone. In the off season he played in intercity competition on the winning team. It was not until the fifth game of the season in his senior year that my brother's name was called for the starting line-up. It was a tremendous season for the team and for my brother. There are five plaques on the wall in the family room of which we are all proud: Most Improved Player, Best Free Throw Percentage, Most Consistent Attitude, Student Athlete Award, Manhood Award."

A young woman, who exemplified the spirit of aliveness, wrote of her family's celebrating the moments of their lives. "We even celebrate 'bar or bat mitzvah' for each child when he or she comes of age. It doesn't matter that we are not Jewish, nor does it matter that my sisters and I are girls. What matters is our family's coming together to celebrate. In this case we celebrate the coming of age, and the responsibilities of young adulthood. My father presents the boy or girl, as the case may be, with a walking stick. A party follows with cake and ice cream. My parents are very positive people. This is an example of the kind of positive action that I have known in my family. It has made us happy people, and we in turn reach out to others."

Objective: To determine positive actions to improve my self-image Exercise/Journal Sheet

ARE YOU IN CONTROL OF YOUR LIFE?

Are you satisfied with yourself? Consider the following areas, and list at least one positive action you can take to improve your self-image.

1. Academically:

2. Physically:

3. As a son/daughter:

4. As a sister/brother:

5. As a friend:

6. As my own person:

7. In the use of my talents:

WRITE A SHORT ESSAY: Recall an incident in your life or one that you have witnessed where one person's positive actions did make a difference in their own/others' lives.

TOPIC: _____ DATE: _____

4 STUDENT STRESS

OBJECTIVES:

1. To discuss the causes of teenage stress
2. To determine my stress as measured by stress tests
3. To evaluate the amount of stress I have experienced
4. To share meaningful ways of coping with stress
5. To discuss stress from worry, fear, and rejection

An original poem written for and read to the class by a very sensitive young man defines well the many areas of student stress.

>Where do I fit in the shape of things?
>   How will I know?
>What will I be ten years from now?
>   Will my hard work show?
>
>Dare I take a glance at the future—
>   career decisions expected today.
>I'm doing my best to get through high school;
>   college seems so far away.
>
>Whose expectations are greater: parents' or friends'?
>   Peers' demands are now.
>Parents want their offspring to be successful,
>   if only we knew how.
>
>What meaning will a distinguished career have
>   with no one to share?
>Dating from one week to the next is hard,
>   let alone a lifetime of care.
>
>Who should I support in the politics?
>   Is it right for the poor to pay?
>But what if I prosper at the cost of others,
>   will my back be turned that day?
>
>How large a part will religion play?
>   Is money my only Lord?
>Will I be able to see through material problems
>   and really hear His Word?
>
>Why must those so close to me die
>   be a fact that I must bear?
>Enough bombs to blow up the face of the earth,
>   the future is so unclear.
>
>But those teenagers who have no confusion
>   haven't really lived.
>More can be learned from these experiences
>   than they can ever give.

STUDENT STRESS AND WHAT TO DO ABOUT IT

We know a restlessness as youth that denies the uniqueness of our being and hurries past the beauty that surrounds us. Childhood is so short, and too soon we are expected to develop an understanding mentally and emotionally that befits our physical growth. So much is expected of us at home, at school, on the job: by our parents, by our teachers, our friends, and our employers. So many questions go unanswered. There is so much doubt and confusion about: Who am I? What is life? How are we to determine in a few short high school years the direction for our lives that will bring fulfillment to us and satisfaction to our parents? These pressures and worries are the fundamental causes of student stress.

Many students have added causes of stress that have been brought about through the divorce of their parents. No other single factor causes as much worry, fear, and stress as the break up of a family.

Family pride runs deep at the cost of bottled-up feelings. When people deny release to pent-up emotions, their inner stress takes away their freedom to be themselves.

STUDENT DISCUSSION/ESSAY

A mature young woman opens the discussion with very few words. "I am now living with my third stepfather."

A vivacious young woman tells of developing a humor mask as a cover for the stress in her life since the divorce of her parents. "Many times I make people laugh to cover my feelings. Since my parents' divorce there is no longer a sense of family tranquillity. Instead there is a kind of fighting or arguing going on most of the time. I don't talk about family problems or my personal problems; I prefer to work them out myself."

"Money is the cause of greatest stress for me," admitted a shy girl. "I am going to Florida with a group of my friends over Spring Break. My parents are paying for my ticket and will give me spending money. But I feel so guilty in not contributing. You see, my parents won't let me get a part-time job. They say that I don't need to work. But if I had my own money, I wouldn't have to be so accountable."

"I can understand what you're saying. I have a job, but sometimes the money I make runs out before I get paid again. One of my most stressful times is having to ask my dad for gas money. I get the money, but I get a lecture along with it. I hate to have to explain."

"My greatest stress comes just before report cards are due, especially if I haven't been studying and I know that my grades will be low," confessed Herb. "It makes me feel like a whole different person when I am under stressful conditions."

In a young man's journal, causes of stress were paired with identity: "As a son: any kind of confrontation. Coping: making sure I have a job and live up to my parents' expectations. As a student: school work, tests, and grades. Coping: doing my homework. As a teen: girl/boy relationships. I always need signs that they still like me as much as I like them, or I ask. As an employee: getting the job done. I try to please my boss."

A young woman's essay summarizes student stress: "Stress is a major problem in today's society. It can cause heart problems, high blood pressure, or depression. The trouble is that it's difficult to get rid of it. It seems that almost any situation can be stressful. For me, school causes the most stress. Many demands and responsibilities are pushed on me. I expect a lot from myself and this adds to the pressure. I'm constantly worrying about grades. Diet is also a cause for stress in my life. I have terrible eating habits and have a hard time dealing with my weight problem. One other cause for stress is dealing with people. I'm most comfortable when I'm alone; there is no pressure from other people. I'm very nervous and quiet around unfamiliar people because I fear rejection. Coping with stress is difficult for me. I complain a lot, however; it doesn't help and I usually end up getting my chores done. When the pressure is from school work, I sit down and do it, just to get it out of the way. Sometimes, I eat or cry because of stress, but that's not coping with it. Music and vigorous exercise make for a good release from tension. I have many nervous habits that appear when I'm dealing with people. Cracking my knuckles, blushing, and fidgety hands are just a few. Stress is like another emotion for me. It's always there, and I have to deal with it."

EVALUATION OF STUDENT STRESS

Under stressful conditions, we don't feel in control of ourselves. Stress acts as an inner burden that keeps us from enjoying life and living life to the fullest. The types of pressure vary, but the common linkage is the fact that stress does play a big part in our lives. The serious effects of stress are an underlying reason for identifying the areas of stress in our lives.

We can minimize our risk of illness, experts believe, by being aware of times of high pressure, and taking precautions during these periods.

Clinical psychologists Thomas H. Holmes and R. M. Rahe developed a method of correlating the effects of life changes with illness. From their research, they devised the *Social Readjustment Rating Scale,* which "...assigns numerical values to various events, or life changes, that are common in our lives....The higher the score on the rating scale the greater the person's susceptibility to physical and psychological illness..." (Townsend, 1955).

Martin B. Marx modified the Holmes/Rahe rating scale to include stressful life changes common to teenagers. Dr. Marx, associate professor of community medicine at the University of Kentucky, based his scale on stress data as recorded by the Class of 1976 at Kentucky as they entered from high school. Marx reported that teenage respondents scored much higher on the scale than adults surveyed by Holmes. A score of 300 or more on the Holmes adult scale would represent a major life crisis, and imply the possibility of a high rate of illness. Marx's study found the average teenage stress score to be 900; a score beyond 1,000 indicated the student had experienced a major life change. Though students proved more able to handle this stress, they showed the same tendency as adults to get sick following periods of high stress (Marx, 1975).

Students in the seminar asked to develop their own stress test using a scale of 1–10 ranking. The major life changes found on the Marx Test are primary causes of stress. The students proposed other secondary causes for stress that they knew from their own experience.

Objective: *To evaluate personal stress as determined by taking a stress test*   PROJECT SHEET

HOW MUCH STRESS HAVE YOU EXPERIENCED?

Social Readjustment Rating Scale *

The following table ranks life changes in order of the amount of stress they cause. For each time one of the events has happened in your life in the past years, circle the stress value.

EVENT	Stress Points	EVENT	Stress Points
Death of spouse	100	Change/financial state	38
Divorce (you, parents)	73	Changing participation in courses	38
Pregnancy (or cause of)	68	Death of close friend	37
Marital separation	65	Change different/work	36
Jail term	63	Change in number of arguments with mate	35
Death of family, friend	63		
Broken engagement	60	Trouble with in-laws	29
Engagement	55	Outstanding achievement	28
Personal injury/illness	53	Mate begins/stops work	26
Marriage	50	Begin or end school	26
Entering college	50	Change in living conditions	20
Varying independence or responsibilities	50	Revision of personal habits	24
		Change in work/hrs/conditions	20
Conflict/change in values	50	Change in residence	20
Drug use	49	Change in schools	20
Fired at work	47	Change in recreation	19
Change/use of alcohol	47	Change in church activities	19
Reconciliation w/mate	45	Change in social activity	18
Trouble School Admin.	45	Going into debt	17
Change in health (family)	44	Change in sleeping habits	16
Working + school	42	Change in frequency of family gatherings	15
Change course of study	40		
Sex difficulties	39	Change in eating habits	13
Change dating habits	39	Vacation	13
Gain new family member	39	Christmas	12
Business readjustments	39	Minor violation w/law	11

* Thomas H. Holmes and R. M. Rahe, 1967 (from *Psychiatric Mental Health Nursing*, Mary C. Townsend, 1993).

Student stress score:_____

Class stress score average:_____

PROJECT SHEET

CAUSES OF STRESS: A STUDENT EVALUATION

Evaluate each on a scale of 1–10:

1. Death of a parent _____
2. Close friend/family member moves away _____
3. Uptight parents _____
4. Time pressure:
   Being on time _____
   Reports done on time _____
5. Parents' divorce _____
6. Athletic team _____
7. Unemployment:
   Family member _____
   Self _____
8. Boredom, loneliness _____
9. Grades or tests _____
10. Car ownership _____
11. Traffic violation or accident _____
12. Messenger of bad news to parents _____
13. Important dates:
    Birthday _____
    Prom _____
    Christmas _____

14. Family obligation to "go as a family" _____
15. Household chores _____
16. Lack of sleep _____
17. Career decision _____
18. College acceptance _____
19. Job pressure _____
20. Financial pressure _____
21. Weight/dieting _____
22. Peer pressure _____
23. Absenteeism, make-up work _____
24. Drugs/alcohol _____
25. Making decisions _____
26. Speaking in front of others _____
27. Being accepted by peers _____
28. Making a date with opposite sex _____

Tally your score: _____

Class average: _____

Objectives: To identify causes of stress in my life
To discuss the cause of teenage stress and means of coping
To evaluate the amount of stress already experienced

EXERCISE/JOURNAL SHEET

STUDENT STRESS AND WHAT TO DO ABOUT IT

Comment on each of the following:

1. In which identity do you experience the most stress? Why? How do you cope?

2. Consider the primary causes of stress in your life as suggested by your score on "How Much Stress Have You Experienced?"

3. Consider the secondary causes of stress in your life as suggested by your score on "Causes of Stress: A Student Evaluation."

WRITE A SHORT ESSAY evaluating the causes of stress in your life. Cite examples. Relate how you cope.

TOPIC: _____ DATE: _____

STRESS FROM WORRY, FEAR, AND REJECTION

ARE YOU A WORRY WART?

As young people we sometimes worry about the future, not allowing ourselves to enjoy the present day. Our foremost category of worry is as a son/daughter. In this identity, worry centers around the desire for parental approval coupled with the desire to be accepted for ourselves. There is the worry of parents overreacting and not trusting our choice of friends, or not respecting our decision in the choice of a job, or in our choice of participating in a particular sport or extracurricular activity.

Worrying ahead of time about leaving home, making new friends, and doing well in college is voiced by many. The decisions regarding what to do with our lives and our career choices weigh heavily on us, as well as the ever-nagging question of success.

As teenagers, students worry about being accepted. They voice concern about their friends, and the loneliness in leaving friends to go to college. They speak of the worry of being able to do things that they believe in, of getting a good job, of making enough money. Others speak of more personal worries about their weight, being shy, and being understood.

Life does not answer our questions. Rather it is up to each of us to answer life's questions for ourselves. The best possible solutions to life's many questions is to learn to know oneself, to accept oneself, and to love oneself. When we love ourselves we are energized and open to challenge. We should accept life's problems on a daily basis and look for solutions within ourselves.

Some people get in the habit of worrying. Any change, any new situation, new person, or new idea is stress filled. This type of worry is true of old people, who probably worry because they feel helpless. But young people should make life an adventure by welcoming change and growing with it.

Young people who admit to extended worry should develop a new attitude about themselves and about life. They might start believing in themselves as persons. They might take the attitude "I can do it," and give it a try in reaching out to others and to new challenges. To do this a person has to try, and sometimes try again. But if a person is trying, that person is doing something about the situation. Worry has never accomplished one positive thing. If a person fills his or her mind with expectations, looks for beauty, welcomes a friend, or does a good deed, there won't be time for worry.

STUDENT DISCUSSION/ESSAY

A mature young man signaled to start the discussion. "I'm the oldest child in my family, and my father frequently travels long distances by plane. I have often thought, 'What if my Dad were to die? What would happen to all of my hopes and dreams for my future?' I would feel responsible for taking care of my mom and my brothers and sisters."

Jessica of her situation: "It's just Mom and me at my house. As I was growing up, I wanted my mother to be all mine. Now I realize that perhaps I have created a handicap. I worry that my mom won't want to let me go."

"I worry about my grades, living up to my parents' expectations, and knowing success," confided Erin.

"I worry about completing my assignments on time, getting good grades, or getting grades good enough to graduate. I am also anxious about being accepted into college." Emily nervously studied her hands.

Ben spoke up. "Emily, I share your worries, and I'll add one more. My parents expect me to be accepted into the college of their choice!"

"Right on. Right on!" someone exclaimed.

"And I'll add one more worry to your list, Ben," quipped a spirited class leader. "I worry about leaving home, leaving old friends, and making it on my own."

"I worry about fitting in. When I meet new people, I worry that they won't like me," admitted Jo.

"I worry about making it in college as a student. At this point, I don't even know what I want to do with my life!" Erica shrugged her shoulders with her admission.

A sensitive young man expressed his concerns this way: "What if I study for a career, and then find that I don't like it? Or marry and find that we can't make it work? Or what if I can't live up to my own expectations? Or if I don't make enough money to do the things that I want to do?"

A shy young woman wrote the following in her journal: "Sometimes I think that I think too much. I used to think about how I looked all the time, and my self-confidence was dependent upon how I looked. Now I am not so dependent on the external part of me. Now I'm mostly concerned about mental anxiety. All I seem to do is worry, worry, worry. Most of the time I have a positive attitude, but I am worried about my future. I hope that I can come to terms with my anxiety and use it in a positive manner."

WHAT DO YOU FEAR?

The word *phobia* is defined as a strong, unreasonable, continuing fear of some particular thing or situation. Students, when asked to identify situations where they know fear, and if possible to explain why, made a long list. The responses varied from heights to spiders, to the dark of night, to being alone, to becoming a Yuppie.

We all have choices to make concerning who we are or who we will become. They are everyday kind of choices based upon how we look at life. Students who speak of family and friends as being an intrinsic value to them will not sacrifice that love for gold or glory. They have already been thinking about the choices they will make in terms of the people they want to become.

STUDENT DISCUSSION/ESSAY

"I fear heights. I always have, though I don't know why. I have never admitted this to anyone before," confessed Michael as the discussion opened. "Just yesterday, I had a chance to overcome this fear. When I got home from school, our neighbor was having coffee with my mom The neighbor had locked herself out of her house, and they expected me to put a ladder to a second floor window to get in. I was stress filled, but better that I try it than admit my fear. I chose an open window near a tall tree, just in case. I did it! But I don't know if I conquered the fear. I shake just thinking about it."

"I fear heights, too," laughed Rita. "Maybe it's because I remember Dad holding me on the railing overlooking Niagara Falls. I am still aware of that sensation of fear when I think about it."

"Me?" questioned Ted, when the turn came to him. "I fear the end of girl/guy relationships. It's hard to let go."

An introspective teen said, "I fear change. Any kind of change." Her voice fell, and then she continued, "When I changed schools to come here, it was frightening. Everything was different. There was so much to get used to—people, places, and things. This class has helped me. You are not threatening. I feel accepted."

In her essay a young woman wrote: "I fear becoming a Yuppie! I would hate to be so worried about money that I would fail to enjoy my life. I fear enjoying a career so much that I wouldn't take time for doing the things that I enjoy doing. I have seen this happen to people whom I love. They spend so much time worrying about getting the best job, house, car, etc., but they don't seem to be having much fun, and they aren't fun to be around.... Now, I fear that I will get so involved with my school work that I won't have time for my friends or my family. I worry that maybe while I'm growing up I'll miss some of my nieces' and nephews' growing up. I have seen adults turn into people who were so unlike the persons whom I once knew. Sometimes I wonder if they had turned into what society had wanted them to be."

DO YOU FEAR REJECTION?

In his journal, a boy had written the word *father* as his major area of rejection, and this explanation: "Because I try so hard to please him, and I want him to be proud of me."

Within every identity lies the possibility of rejection. The identities that mean the most to us are the same identities in which rejection is the most damaging. Since most students admit that their desire to please their parents is a top priority, then rejection by a parent is the most devastating.

We all fear rejection, and often curb our activities or actions because we do not want to risk being criticized or misunderstood. Each of us who has been rejected at some point in our lives can still recall the incident, and perhaps the people involved. We can recall, as well, what happened to us, and our feeling of being unwanted or unworthy.

Rejection and the fear of rejection are the most restrictive influences keeping us from reaching out to others and to life. The vulnerability of our ego is the risk faced in rejection. A rejection early in life can often be translated as "not good enough" in other phases of life as well.

We all have felt rejected in our lives and not necessarily because of anything that was said. Feelings of rejection occur when people fail to realize the sensitivity of others or simply do not care how they treat them.

STUDENT DISCUSSION/ESSAY

Karl offered to start the discussion. "I can remember a neighborhood kickball game. We all gathered around the captains who took turns picking one kid after another until just one kid was left—me. I felt rejected because I was one of the guys who wanted to play, and because they felt that I wasn't a good enough player to be on the team." He held in his mind a photographic memory of the incident.

"It was the custom at our school for a Booster Club member to decorate a box in school colors, fill it with treats, and give it to a team member on the day of a game. One player had the audacity to dump his box and its contents into the trash basket in front of the girl who gave it to him!" The students looked at Nancy in disbelief. "Believe it!"

A young woman wrote of a childhood memory: "I remember a situation in which I really felt rejected. My family rarely did things together, mainly because my father was always away (my parents are divorced). One day, though, he took both of my brothers and my sister out, leaving me at home. He took them places and did stuff with them. He even bought them things like candy and toys. Well, when he got home, he didn't bring any for me. Boy, did I feel rejected! I remember crying, but there really wasn't anything that I could do about it."

From a young man's essay. "I felt rejected one time when I asked a girl out. She said yeah at first, but then she started to avoid me, and never returned any of my calls. About a week after I had asked her out, she said that she didn't want to go out. So I said, 'Why did you say yes in the first place?' She said, 'I don't know.' I tried forgetting, but it didn't work. I fear rejection by friends, family and life in general. It hurts. Everyone wants to be accepted."

Objective: To acknowledge insecurities brought about by worry, fear, and rejection

EXERCISE/JOURNAL SHEET

STRESS FROM WORRY, FEAR, AND REJECTION

1. Do you worry a lot? About what?   How do you combat worry?

2. What do you fear?   Do you know the reason?

3. Do you fear rejection?   Why?

WRITE A SHORT ESSAY on one of the topics or **CHOOSE A QUOTE** from the readings. Relate it to yourself or to someone you know. Cite an example.

TOPIC: _____ DATE: _____

Quote from Reading (pp._____) _____

5 GENERATION GAP

OBJECTIVES:

1. To share feelings and concerns regarding relationships with parents
2. To realize remaining time at home is short
3. To make an effort to understand parents
4. To be an instrument of peace at home

VERSE 1: Parental Frustration

    We only see you
        with friends
        and between phone calls.

    We never have time
        for pleasant conversations,
        but much time for shouting
        over the television, the loud music,
        or just over trivial things.

    In your mind, parents are people
        to argue with
        over eating, clothes,
        what time to come in,
        homework, or
        cleaning your room,
        as these are
        the only things done at home.

    There is no time
        for pleasantries...or
        if there is time,
        you seem not to care.

    Your nicer self—
        bright, happy, clever, loving—
        you take off like a coat
        when you enter
        what we call home.

    Home is defined as a hangout
        when you haven't any place
        better to go.
        A hang-up as far as living
        is concerned.
        But it does provide phone
        service, laundry, transportation,
        bed, bag, and a great place to
        rid oneself of frustration.

You may be dreaming great dreams,
> but the door mat
> which we have spent weaving together
> into the pattern
> of our lives, you seem, sometimes,
> to pound with dust.

The only place teenagers have to go
> is up, and why not—
> They knock down all that stands,
> and stand tall
> upon the ruins.

VERSE 2:   Youth Speaks

Try to understand
> what I am
> about to say.

We live together
> and yet
> so far away.

You want me
> to be
> the image
> you didn't achieve.

But I want
> to be
> an example
> of what I believe.

The world has
> shown me
> what money
> can buy...

But no one
> can tell me
> what makes
> a man cry.

When I choose a friend,
> I judge him with care—
> I measure his heart,
> You measure his hair.

When I think of mankind,
    I equate black as white.
    When I call him "brother,"
    you start a fight.

When I look ahead,
    I weigh life with "soul."
    Your drive is success,
    with money the goal.

When I ask a question,
    you won't hear me out.
    You retort in lecture,
    and most often shout.

I cannot remember,
    when you gave me praise.
    It's "hang-up," " turn-down,"
    "do homework"—a maze.

Sometimes, I wonder
    if you really care,
    how I look at life,
    or what dreams I bear.

The original poem, entitled "Generation Gap," was written a generation earlier. It expressed the parental feelings of that time and spoke for the youth as well.

In discussing the basic causes for arguments with parents, trivial things surface:
- responsibility for chores
- use of the phone
- fighting with siblings
- time away from home
- doing homework
- grades
- money problems
- car or absence of
- filling out college applications
- feeding/walking the dog
- going out with whom? where?
- raising my voice

The discussion indicates that the basis for family arguments has not changed, and parents still "yell" at teenagers to get their attention.

WHO STARTS THE ARGUMENTS AT HOME? WHY?

In family discord, is it *who* starts the argument, or *what* starts the argument? The fabric that holds and molds family life has strength and elasticity beyond compare. An acquaintance would no longer acknowledge us, our friends would drop us, if we treated them the way we sometimes deal with family members.

We are going to disagree. We are going to vent our frustrations, and we often do it at home. Many times our anger is misplaced and we take it out on those we love. Once we think about it, we might change our ways.

The most important structure in society is the family unit. Family ties, by their very nature, need to be elastic. The give and take under which most other relationships would crumble actually causes the family to grow more closely knit when love is the prevailing attitude.

STUDENT DISCUSSION/ESSAY

Allen was eager to start the discussion. He said, "The main thing that starts arguments at my house is the stupid little stuff. For example, I am told to clean my room, take out the trash, do something constructive, or shouldn't you be doing your homework? Then it really gets started, and everything that I have or haven't done in the past six months surfaces. Sometimes we can't agree on anything."

"It's usually the little things at my house, too," quipped Ed. "My mother always complains that I don't hang up my coat. I don't understand why she always picks on me. When my dad does the same thing, she simply hangs his coat up, but she just yells at me. I don't think that I've ever started an argument with my mom. She starts them, blames me and drags my dad into it." The honesty of his comments brought laughter.

"I start the arguments," said Josh, "by not doing something that I'm told to do. After my parents remind me again, I'll tell them, 'I know' or I'll give them a smart remark back. It usually ends in a yelling match, and I do the thing that I should have done in the first place." Friendly chuckles followed Josh's statement, too.

"At my house, it is usually my dad," put in Eric. "He yells at me for little things that I do wrong—like spilling something. Then he ties that to something that is unrelated. He likes to stretch the situation into a problem. All in all, though, we get along."

"Most of the time, I cause the arguments at our house," admitted Jill with a smile. "I have been on the phone too long, or I haven't straightened my room. But I wouldn't call them arguments. I just get yelled at, and I know why."

Ashley spoke next. "My parents are the ones who start the arguments. It usually happens when they are tired or have had a bad day at work."

Many students refer to mood swings as contributing to starting arguments with a parent. A thoughtful young woman spoke knowingly: "It depends. If my father is in a bad mood, he will start the argument. The slightest thing will make him mad. Other times I'm the culprit. Most of the time there is no apparent reason. We seem to take our stress or frustration out on each other. It seems to happen less often when we are on vacation, or in situations where we have little stress."

"It's mood related at our house, too," Kate added. "If one of my parents is in a bad mood, and I do something to make that parent mad, we have an argument. One time, I forgot to ask the guidance counselor about my college application. My mom asked me about it, and when I didn't have the answer, she started yelling that I needed to take responsibility for myself. She thinks that I depend on people to do things for me. That is not true! So, I yelled back." She paused, and said with a grin, "They say that I'm disrespectful if I don't respond."

"My parents say that certain jobs were created for men and certain jobs for women. I always argue with them about this attitude. Women are not servants! We are equals with men." Angie was vehement.

"I think that my parents start arguments because of their displaced anger. Someone at work makes them mad, and they come home and take it out on us. On days when I sense that they are upset, I just leave them alone. If I get upset, I might say something I will regret."

An example of student sensitivity is expressed in the following student essay. "Arguments are started by both parent and child. Sometimes they are provoked. However, it may only take one person being in a bad mood, or having a bad day, who will trigger an argument over a trivial comment by a family member.

"Family arguments are sometimes petty but at other times they are important. Family members often express feelings that need to be brought out into the open. The subject may be taboo for the quiet home scene, but one which can surface in the framework of family hostility. Once a subject is broached, thoughts linger in the minds of family members. Time heals. Time also allows all to reconsider their positions, and reaffirm or question their first decisions. It is important that the channels of family communication remain open."

Objective: *To discuss my feelings and concerns associated with teen/parent relationships*

EXERCISE/JOURNAL SHEET

WHO STARTS THE ARGUMENTS AT HOME? WHY?

1. Do you agree with the sentiments expressed? Why?

   Verse 1: Parental Frustration

   Verse 2: Youth Speaks

2. List five trivial things that you and your parent(s) argue about.

   a. _____

   b. _____

   c. _____

   d. _____

   e. _____

3. Who starts the arguments at your house? Explain.

4. Do you feel that too much is expected of you at home? Explain.

WRITE A SHORT ESSAY on one of the topics or CHOOSE A QUOTE from the readings. Relate it to your life or to someone you know. Cite an example.

TOPIC: _____ DATE: _____

Quote from Reading (pp. _____) _____

TRY TO UNDERSTAND YOUR PARENTS

When asked what parents think are important considerations for young people, the students are quick to respond:
- Get a good education.
- Be responsible in your faith.
- Keep the family close.
- Make good friends.
- Spend time at home.
- Stay away from bad influences.
- Be respectable.
- Set goals. Have a desire to achieve in life.
- Avoid drugs and drinking.

Most of us understand that our parents think they are making demands and rules for our own good, but we still want to choose for ourselves. We sometimes don't recognize that parental injunctions are meant as a safety shield from the enticements of the real world. Children are a gift so precious that most parents dedicate their lives to their care, and for this are often misunderstood.

THINGS THAT PARENTS HAVE FORGOTTEN FROM THEIR YOUTH

Do our parents expect more of us than was expected of them as teenagers? Or is it the wisdom of love that seeks to protect and guide the young?

Respect for our parents' wishes is a major issue, and a basis for misunderstandings in family relationships. As young people, we sometimes forget how fleeting our time is in the family scene. Parents, on the other hand, are aware that the guidance needed to last a lifetime is measured in a few short years.

Society changes with each generation. Scientific breakthroughs have brought major changes on the home front as well as on the job. This generation has been called the throwaway generation. Nothing seems permanent. Attitudes and values have been changing. Sex, crime, drug and alcohol abuse, and violence have become part of the teenage scene.

Parents have many worries for their children. They live under the burden of many pressures from their jobs and their family responsibilities. Most parents want the best for their children.

STUDENT DISCUSSION/ESSAY

"They have forgotten that they learned from their mistakes and their own experiences. We want to learn from ours!" Jason was the first to speak out.

"Yes, and at our age there is a feeling of rebellion sometimes. Some might call it curiosity or adventure. I overheard stories my dad told his buddies about when he was young," Joe related.

Susan spoke up. "They have forgotten how hard growing up is with the pressures of falling in love, or fighting with your boyfriend and girlfriends."

"And the pressure we have about grades and college."

"True!" agreed Ellen. "My parents have obviously forgotten how hard it is dealing with the idea of college. They are so busy wanting me to be someone else that they forget who I really am. They forget that I'm not always serious about things, and that I am not an A student! It's important for parents to love kids for who they really are."

"Exactly!" Brett burst in in agreement. "My parents bug me about completing my college applications. I'm half afraid to send them in for fear that I won't be accepted. Then I will really disappoint them."

Marc was next to speak. "My parents have forgotten what being young is like, too. They never go out and have a good time. They have forgotten how to put some romance into their marriage, and this is hurting my social life. They don't want to see me going out all the time. They don't want to see me having a good time while they stay at home."

Sally spoke up. "I don't agree, Marc. I think parents have forgotten how to be young, but I don't think that they begrudge us our good times. My parents don't go out much either. Everything is so expensive. But they are active here at school and at church functions."

"A lot depends on the circumstances," said Dennis. "I don't go out on week nights. I do on weekends. I think my parents are happy to see me have a good time. I work hard and earn my own spending money."

John had a different point to make. "Parents should not compare their high school lives with ours. Times have changed. Growing up today is much more difficult. There are more pressures."

"Agreed," said Rob. "Sometimes when I talk to my parents, they claim to know how it is for us, when really their thoughts are outdated. The best they could do is to offer advice that agrees with the time period. They should not try to be an expert on the situation because if they didn't go through it, they don't know."

A very quiet girl entered the discussion. "What about the pressure to spend quality time at home? Right now, I want to be with my friends. They understand me. I can relax with them, and have some fun. Contrary to what they might think, we are not always up to mischief."

"Sometimes I need to be left alone. I feel that I am an adult, and that I have a right to privacy. I have a lot of pressure on me right now. I've reached the point where I feel I should make my own decisions. My parents should trust me to do the right thing." The young man's words seemed to echo in the minds of those who heard him.

"My dad says that society is very different now than when he went to high school. My grandparents didn't have the worries that my parents have today. My dad is probably older than most of your parents," Penny announced. "He says that drug and alcohol abuse were not a part of his high school scene."

MAKING A CONCERTED EFFORT TO UNDERSTAND YOUR PARENTS

In a very real sense, high school graduation is a step into adulthood. Teenage time with the family is fleeting. We are challenged to discover the impact our actions can have in being an instrument for peace in the family.

We have discussed the trouble with parents. We have named a few of the innumerable trivial incidents in a day that can provoke an argument between us and a parent. One might think that parents were held in no regard, until we are caught short by students who have lost a parent to death or divorce.

STUDENT DISCUSSION/ESSAY

Rose was the first to speak. "I used to be unsure of my parents' love for each other. But lately, I can see it clearly. We have had a very difficult four years financially due to my dad's job change. Recently, I see Mom living like it doesn't have to be bad. During these years our lives changed a great deal. But Mom never complained, and she wouldn't stand for anyone undercutting Dad."

Ben raised his hand to speak next. "Every day I make a conscious effort to get along with my father. We are completely different people with completely different goals. I have a hard time living with a family where the father is in complete control. He is the only one who makes the decisions. He believes that children are to be seen and not heard. I disagree with his attitude, and it is constantly causing friction between us. How do I handle this?"

"Think ahead and do something nice for him. Surprise him," offered Margot. "Everyone reacts well to a kindness. I'll bet you find he has a good heart." Ben nodded with a smile.

"My parents were divorced when I was still young," Nicole said. "As time went on, they recovered from the transition, but I felt torn between them. Both parents would use me as a go-between. I started to hate my father. As I grew older, I learned to deal with my feelings of resentment. I get along better with him now, but that could be because he recently moved to Florida.... My mother feels that she has to do her best, and this includes my getting accepted into college. My mom didn't go to college. Now I must succeed, so that she can succeed!"

"My parents are also divorced," said Carol. "My dad totally ignores me and the rest of the family. I think my mom is overprotective. She doesn't understand that in today's world it's okay for a girl to call a boy. It's hard for her, feeling so responsible for us. It's hard on us, too."

Todd spoke up. "I tried to live with my mother after my parents were divorced. But we could never get along when it came to my social life. She would just say, 'No, you can't go.' She would not give me a reason, and we would fight. I finally moved in with my father."

"I don't think that I have ever made a conscious effort to get along with my parents," admitted Ted. "On the other hand, many times I try not to say what I am thinking, so I won't start an argument. At other times, I do little things just so a bad result won't occur. These are my ways of getting along with my parents."

"I'd like to tell about a happy time with my parents," Nick offered. "It was when interim report cards came out. I knew that I was failing two classes at the end of that quarter, and I knew that my parents were really mad. But they were willing to listen. I told them that I was sorry, and that I would bring my grades up. They seemed to understand my feelings. I did improve my grades. Their understanding of me made it easier for me to understand them."

"Being an instrument of peace at home means doing as I am told, not teasing my brothers and sister, doing my homework, and getting good grades. These actions do make our house more peaceful." Jerry laughed nervously with his admission.

"When I express my love and gratitude to my parents for all they mean to me, I am making a conscious effort to make them happy. I should do it more often. I should tell them every day," explained Marty.

"I agree with Marty. I think that we as teenagers don't appreciate our parents as much as we should. When we are at home we can either cause or prevent trouble. Each of us knows what we can do to keep our parents happy. We also know how to get them upset and angry. The same is true, of course, of our parents. We should let them know that we appreciate them."

"I always tried to get along with my parents, but life became difficult when my mother died. My dad trusts me. He gives me many responsibilities, and he lets me do whatever I want, as long as I am safe," said Jonathan, who usually didn't speak up.

In an essay, a hostile junior wrote out his feelings on the topic of understanding parents. "I get along with my parents, as long as I follow their rules. I try my best to do things the way they like. They think that I have no responsibilities. I think that going to school every day is a responsibility. My parents don't see the effort and time it takes just staying in school.

"Parents see drugs, sex and alcohol, but they would never think their own children would get involved. Some people stay away from that stuff, but it is out there and a lot of people are involved. I think it is wrong when our parents expect us to be perfect individuals—always having good grades and never doing anything wrong. I do appreciate the things I have. I do believe that I am well taken care of. I also think that my parents appreciate me, but sometimes they get sidetracked." Jeff had given his essay a great deal of thought.

A very sensitive student wrote the following beautiful essay, which put the student discussions in perspective. He wrote: "Getting along with your parents and making an effort to understand them can build your relationship with them. By building your relationship, you become more appreciated at home. The more you contribute to the good of the family, the better your life will be.

"Parents should also try to remember what it was like for them and their parents when they were teenagers. Finally, we should not be afraid to speak out at home, because our opinions will be appreciated. The most important part of family life is the input of all members and being comfortable with our family."

Objectives: *To realize teenage time at home is short*
To share ways of understanding parents
To be an instrument of peace at home

EXERCISE/JOURNAL SHEET

TRY TO UNDERSTAND YOUR PARENTS

1. What have your parents forgotten from their youth?

2. What do your parents think are important considerations for your generation?

3. List five trivial things that can make your parents happy.

   a. _____

   b. _____

   c. _____

   d. _____

   e. _____

4. Have you ever made a conscious effort to get along with your parents? Explain.

5. How can you be an instrument of peace in your home?

WRITE A SHORT ESSAY on one of the topics or CHOOSE A QUOTE from the readings. Relate it to yourself. Cite an example.

TOPIC: _____ DATE: _____

Quote from Reading (pp._____) _____

6   THERE IS NO ONE TO LISTEN

OBJECTIVES:

1. To define loneliness for myself
2. To share the many faces of loneliness
3. To discuss ways to overcome loneliness
4. To understand loneliness as a part of being human

A guidance counselor tells of a sophomore who asked, "What is the name of the course where everyone listens to what someone has to say? I'd like to take that course. It meets in the open area, in the Art Gallery."

The pensive student who asked the question was referring to an elective course, where students discussed how they looked at themselves, at others, and at life. "In that moment," the counselor relates, "I realized the significance of this discussion course from a different perspective—that of a lonely boy. He had stopped by after school one day to say, 'My grandmother is coming this weekend. I hope that I get to see her, but she doesn't like my stepmother.' I've thought about his statement in conjunction with characteristic signs of anxiety that I had observed in him—an anxiety that overshadows his learning ability."

LONELINESS FOR ME

The floodgates of thought seem to open as we share perceptions of loneliness. The breadth of the spectrum is like the arch of a huge rainbow in its reach across the horizon of our lives.

Each of us has known loneliness many times, in many different ways, for loneliness is a part of all our lives. It reaches from the small child to the very aged. No one can escape its pain.

The dictionary defines *lonely* as "unhappy at being alone." Loneliness, then, is being alone when we don't want to be. Life goes on and we must learn to cope. Part of our maturing is getting to know ourselves. When we are lonely, we should experience the pain of loneliness and use the quiet time to get to know ourselves. With a little practice, we might discover how nice we are to be with!

As we look forward to time alone—to study, to work on a hobby, to read, weight lift—we will discover ourselves through new interests. These interests add new facets to our lives, facets we can enjoy, and will be able to share with another in building a strong relationship. We can choose to be lonely or we can choose to do something about overcoming our loneliness. It's up to each of us to decide for ourselves what we do with our lives.

People who are successful do something about their loneliness. They accept who they are, and learn to overcome what they cannot change. We should all work toward becoming the person that we want to be.

STUDENT DISCUSSION/ESSAY

The opening statements on loneliness are brief:

"I feel alone a lot."

"I feel lonely after an argument with my parents."

Then a young woman who seemed to know herself well decided to be specific. "I've always been a loner. In grade school, the kids always made fun of me. I didn't fit in. I didn't try to fit in. If they wouldn't stop their insults, I would just think to myself, 'Someday, I'll be a great artist or musician or something, and they will see how wrong they were to treat me this way.' I hold my cat and I feel better."

A quiet youth who usually passed up his turn to speak said, "When I feel lonely, I sit with my dog and watch television in the dark." This boy had been sent to our school from another school district in the hope that he could adjust to other students. Unaware of the social worker's report, a classmate handed him an envelope as he came into class one day, saying, "I thought of you when I saw this." Rich hurriedly opened the envelope, and smiled as he read the card ('Best Friends' was written under the picture of a boy and his dog). "Thanks, Alonzo."

Jenny spoke of a memory she has: "When I was in the eighth grade, I often felt left out. If I didn't go along with what other kids wanted to do, they ignored me. They had different values."

From across the circle, Terry added his comment. "I've been odd man out in a crowd, too. It's tough. I think that one of the greatest fears is to be lonely."

"It's lonely being goalie on the soccer field."

"Yeah, and on the football field, when it's up to you!"

"My grandma is in a nursing home. We visit her on Sunday after church. When I think of loneliness, I think of old people. There are so many at the nursing home who seem to be forgotten."

"I think of the elderly, too, Joe. I have a great aunt who lives alone. I clean her apartment once a week. She follows me around, and is always correcting me on the way I do things. I know she is lonely. But I hate to go there." Sara spoke out, honestly.

Then Margaret motioned to share. She read a poem:

A Crabbit Old Woman Wrote This

"What do you see, employees, what do you see?
What are you thinking when you are looking at me:
A crabbit old woman, and not very wise,
Uncertain of habit, with far away eyes,
Who dribbles her food and makes no reply
When you say in a loud voice, 'I do wish you'd try.'
Who seems not to notice the things that you do,
And forever is losing a stocking or shoe.
Who resisting or not lets you do as you will,
With bathing and feeding, the long day to fill.
Is that what you're thinking, is that what you see?
Then open your eyes, you're not looking at me.
I'll tell you who I am, as I sit there so still,
As I rise at your bidding, as I sit at your will.
I'm a small child of ten with a father and mother,
Brothers and sisters who love one another.
A young girl of sixteen with wings on her feet;
Dreaming that soon her lover she'll meet;
A bride soon at twenty—my heart gives a leap
Remembering the vows that I promised to keep;
At twenty-five now, I have young of my own,
Who need me to build a secure happy home.

A woman of thirty, my young now grow
   fast,
Bound to each other with ties that should
   last.
At forty, my young sons have grown and
   have gone,
But my man is beside me to see I don't
   mourn.
At fifty, once more babies play 'round my
   knee,
Again we know children, my loved one and
   me.
Dark days are upon me, my husband is
   dead,
I look to the future. I shudder with dread.
For my young are all rearing young of
   their own,
And I think of the years and love that I've
   known.
I'm an old woman now and nature is cruel.
'Tis her jest to make old age look like a
   fool.
The body is crumbled, grace and vigor de-
   part,
There now is a stone where I once had a
   heart.
But in this old carcass a young girl still
   dwells
And now and again my battered heart
   swells.
I remember the joys, I remember the pain,
I'm loving and living life over again.
I think of the years all too few—gone too
   fast,
And accept the stark fact that nothing can
   last.
So open your eyes, open and see
Not a crabbit old woman, look closer—see
   me."

Everyone had listened closely. As Margaret put down her paper, she said, "My sister gave me this poem when I started to work with the elderly at a nursing home. The author is unknown. The poem was found among the possessions of an old woman who died in the geriatric ward of Ashleudie Hospital, near Dundee, East Scotland."

"Even babies get lonely," Debbie observed. "I know this, because I babysit. I have seen tears when a mother leaves, and the joy when she returns."

Tony offered a different insight. He spoke up in a serious tone. "Sometimes I need to get to know myself better. For that I need some quiet time and space. I need to be alone. Even alone, I am not lonely. I figure God is always with me."

Kathleen put in, "I don't like to be alone. I like to have a lot of friends because I don't like to be lonely either."

"May I speak?" asked Meg. "I know what Kathy means. I've been lonely when I'm home alone. The sounds of the furnace creaking give me the chills. I can hardly imagine that feeling lasting longer than ten hours! But for some people it does."

"Being lonely. Being alone. These are not the same, and yet could they be?" Beth mused.

"When I feel bad inside, no matter how hard I try to make others understand me, they can't. Then I feel lonely," Kristi said thoughtfully.

A very sensitive young teen raised her hand to speak. "My experience is similar to yours, Kristi. I have become aware that things I say may be misinterpreted by others. I am conscious of this because a good friend of mine often says things to me which hurt me deeply. It has happened many times, and I, too, have felt very much alone. I wonder if she realizes how much pain she has caused me by her insensitive remarks."

"I would say something to her, if she were my friend!" was the spontaneous response of a classmate.

When the discussion came his way, Matt said, "When I think of loneliness, I recall a story that a minister told. It was about a boy who was born out of wedlock, a boy who didn't know who his father was. He and his mother were poor and lived in a small mountain town in Tennessee.

"When he started school his classmates made fun of him, so he went off by himself at recess and during lunch. As he got older, he always felt that people were looking at him. He felt that they wondered, as he did, who his real father was.

"When he was twelve a new preacher came to his church. The boy always slipped in late and slipped out early. But one day he got caught and had to walk out with the crowd. He felt that every eye was on him. Suddenly, he felt a big hand on his shoulder. When he looked up, the preacher was looking right at him and asked 'Who are you, son? Whose boy are you?'

"The boy was so frightened that he didn't answer. He felt that even the preacher was putting him down. But the preacher began to smile. 'Wait a minute,' he said. 'I know who you are. I see the family resemblance. You are a son of God!' With that he slapped him across the back and said, 'Boy, you have a great inheritance. Go and claim it.'

"It's a true story. The boy was Ben Hooper, who was elected to serve two terms as governor of Tennessee."

Objectives: *To define loneliness for myself* EXERCISE/JOURNAL SHEET
To share the many faces of loneliness
To discuss ways to overcome loneliness

LONELINESS FOR ME

1. Bring in something written, remembered, or witnessed that defines loneliness for you.

2. Explain why you may feel lonely as a

   a. Family member

   b. Student

   c. Teenager

4. Do you feel lonely when you are alone? Explain.

5. How do you overcome loneliness?

WRITE A SHORT ESSAY on one of the topics or CHOOSE A QUOTE from the readings. Cite an example. Include your reactions.

TOPIC: _____ DATE: _____

Quote from Reading (pp._____) _____

LONELINESS, A PART OF BEING HUMAN

We all know that loneliness exists. All kinds of people are lonely and ignored in school, at work, in positions of power, and in marriages. Loneliness exists in the homes of the wealthy as well as the homes of the poor. Loneliness exists in the hearts of all people who fail to take responsibility for themselves.

When we appreciate the fact that loneliness is a part of being human, we are more open to reflect on its condition in our own lives.

One way to overcome loneliness is to reach out to someone, and be a means of spreading joy by something as simple as saying hello, or offering to help. By sharing our gifts of time and caring, we also share in others' joy.

Dr. M. Scott Peck speaks of this phenomenon in his book *The Road Less Traveled*.

> ...love is a strangely circular process. For the process of extending one's self is an evolutionary process. When one has successfully extended one's limits, one has grown into a larger state of being. Thus the act of love is an act of self-evolution even when the purpose of the act is someone else's growth. It is through reaching toward evolution that we evolve.

Eugene C. Kennedy writes eloquently about the human condition. In his book *Loneliness and Everyday Problems*, he states that only human beings get painfully lonely. In his definition of loneliness, Kennedy states that a fundamental sign of what it means to be lonely is our need to make contact with other humans. He further contends that the experience of loneliness makes us aware of our incompleteness and motivates us to find ourselves in knowing others.

Some students find it easier to write out their feelings than to express them aloud within the group. Quotations taken from Kennedy's book on loneliness provide the subject matter for student essays.

STUDENT DISCUSSION/ESSAY

"Our capacity for loneliness is the reverse side of our desire for friendship."

One youth wrote, "If our desire for friendship is not met, our capacity for loneliness becomes greater. In the seventh grade, I really liked a girl. But she wouldn't go out with me, because I was a nerd. I did everything to change my image. I listened to popular music and stopped caring about my homework. I tried to change myself, because I didn't like myself. Not liking myself, I had problems having other people like me. Then I came to a school where I didn't know anyone. I'm not good at making friends, so I haven't. At lunch I sit at different tables all the time, because I don't feel like I belong. All of my friends from my old school have lost contact with me. I never do anything with my classmates. Now I don't feel that I belong anywhere."

The lonely sophomore probably thought that he was the only person who felt as he did, and yet in another essay a young woman wrote: "Being without friends and being new to your school is about the loneliest one can get.... Love makes loneliness disappear. A feeling of acceptance is one feeling of love. That is why friends are so important."

An insightful student wrote in her essay: "Many people feel that if they have friends they will never be lonely, but some people who have friends are still lonely."

"We must learn to be friends to ourselves if we wish to be good to others."

Addressing this quotation, one student wrote: "I feel that I must learn to understand myself and be honest with myself. I have many friends, but I am not really sure of our relationships. I'm confused as to why I feel the way I do about this. I guess I must try to figure myself out first, before others try; then I can have a closer, more trusting relationship with friends."

A compassionate young woman wrote: "If you are not able to love and appreciate yourself for who you are, it is hard for others to love you. If you do not have confidence in yourself, it shows, and other people will notice it, too. You must learn to be your own best friend, overlook your flaws, and be the best you can be. Then, after you have helped yourself, you can move on to help others love themselves. You can begin to love them for who they are by overlooking their flaws, and love them for being the best they can be."

From another essay, "...I once knew a girl who had low self-esteem. She didn't care what happened to her. One day, a friend got so upset with the way she was treating herself that the friend spoke out to her. After that, the girl who was once lonely and without love from herself and others gained a new outlook on her life."

"For many people who are lonely in... a marriage relationship... the basic failure is communication."

A pretty girl wrote with conviction: "I have a friend who is also my boyfriend. This past weekend we had our first serious communication problem in over two years. It scares me because if I don't have him to talk to and be open with, I don't know what I will do. I love him, and I love our relationship, and I want it to stay open and honest!"

A thoughtful student wrote: "A lonely person who marries for just the reason of loneliness may end up more lonely from the longing for love in her heart."

A perceptive young man wrote: "I have witnessed many divorces in my life that have resulted from the lack of communication. I think instead of having a divorce, the two people should learn to communicate with each other and work out their problems, either together or with a third party."

Virtually the same sentiments were expressed by another student who concluded, "...you really need to get to know the other person before you get into a commitment."

Finally, from a short essay that carried a most poignant message. "Loneliness is a disease, when you have no one to love or if you aren't loved. Maybe someone is new in town and has no friends. People may ignore him before getting to know him."

Objective: To understand loneliness as a part of being human   EXERCISE/JOURNAL SHEET

LONELINESS, A PART OF BEING HUMAN

Comment on each of the following quotations taken from Eugene C. Kennedy's book *Loneliness and Everyday Problems*.

1. "Our capacity for loneliness is the reverse side of our desire for friendship."

2. "We must learn to be friends to ourselves if we wish to be good to others."

3. "For many people who are lonely in . . . a marriage relationship . . . the basic failure is communication."

4. ". . . peace comes for those who are willing to work at deepening their overall relationship with each other."

5. "In our longing for meaning there is an uneasiness at doing something we do not entirely believe in."

WRITE A SHORT ESSAY on one of the topics or CHOOSE A QUOTE from the readings. Cite an example. Relate it to your life, or one you have witnessed.

TOPIC: _____ DATE: _____

Quote from Reading (pp._____) _____

7   FRIENDSHIP

OBJECTIVES:

1. To acknowledge the importance of friendship
2. To share ideas on the meaning of friendship
3. To share interpretations of famous quotations on friendship

FRIENDSHIP'S MEANING TO ME

> "A lot of people know the surface side of me, the side they see while I'm working, or just through the day. But there is another side of me—an inside that people never see. The inside of me has so many moods that the outside never shows.
>
> "It is a part that is full of a thousand thoughts; a part that embraces love and cherishes friendships; a part that understands without need for words; a part that has yearnings, desires, and prayers.
>
> "For once in my life, I trust someone implicitly, and I care about someone in a totally understanding way. I feel like it's okay to let someone in—someone like you—to let myself be seen emotionally and physically as who I really am. I have told you things that I've never told another soul.
>
> "I trust you with my secrets, and you know now that you can trust me with yours. This sharing, this special sharing, is one of the nicest dimensions my life has ever known."

The fun-loving, vivacious teen who wrote this beautiful essay in her journal never chose to share her deeper thoughts in class discussions. How blessed she and her friend are. Just to know that so lovely a relationship exists makes the world seem a brighter place.

Friendship is an intrinsic treasure, always. It is valued most greatly during teenage years, when young people have so much to learn about themselves and about life. Their need to be understood is never greater than in these formative years, when the knowledge of acceptance is a wellspring of courage and hope.

"The journey out of loneliness into love begins when we take the risk of letting another person know us. Know our fears and our failures, pain and sorrow. If someone stands with us through our pain then we can believe that we are loved." This quotation is from the book *From Loneliness to Love,* in which the authors, Douglas Morrison and Christopher Witt, express so well the universal need for friendship.

STUDENT DISCUSSION/ESSAY

Discussion of friendship begins with students sharing what speaks of friendship to them.

"Friendship is a special bond made up of special things."

"Friendship is everything."

Several students brought in photos and passed them around as they spoke with pride of their friends. One young man opened his wallet and from a plastic card-holder took out a well-worn picture of Christ, saying as he held it up to be seen, "*He* is my friend."

Now the discussion began in earnest. An enthusiastic cheerleader said, "When you are with close friends, you are complete as yourself."

A thoughtful senior remarked, "When you find someone who fits the friend picture, and you can see that she cares, you must hold on and never let her go."

Betsy was next to comment. "Good friends bring out the best in people, and maybe something they are not when they are not with that friend—like different interests and hobbies. A good friend helps you become a better person."

Tess added, "Friends are people to be happy and joyous with."

"What makes friendship special is the choosing to be with that person," a thoughtful young man declared.

"Friendship can't be just when it's convenient. It has to be all the time, with no strings attached," John asserted.

Amy spoke up, choosing her words carefully. "Friends are people we love for what they are, not who they are."

"For me, friendship is being yourself when you are with the other person," offered Jodie.

"I agree!" said Marty. "That's what friendship is all about—being yourself when you are with a friend, not something everyone wants you to be. People shouldn't have to lie to be liked by others. People should be themselves."

Jeff spoke up: "There's this girl I like right now and she feels the same. When I am with her I don't have to put on an act—act macho. I can be who I really am. I can tell her anything, and she'll be there telling me, 'It's all right.'"

"Amen. To have a true relationship, people have to be honest. They have to be in touch with themselves. I can't stand fakes," Chris said, and he meant it.

Lauren shared her thoughts: "In all friendships, be it boy-girl, girl-girl, or boy-boy, a lot of how you begin to love someone is how that person makes you feel. If your friend is positive with you, it's easier to be a little more positive about yourself. Having a friend makes it easy to risk sharing something of yourself."

Francie waved her hand to speak next. "What attracts me to another person is how I feel when we are together. If I feel good with someone, I want to be around that person more and more, not to build up my ego, but to receive and give positive feelings. So many times, it is not how great the other person is, but how great you feel when you are with him or her."

Objectives: To acknowledge the importance of friendship
To share ideas on the meaning of friendship

EXERCISE/JOURNAL SHEET

FRIENDSHIP'S MEANING TO ME

1. Bring in something written, remembered, or saved that speaks of friendship to you.

2. Recall an act of friendship that you hold in memory.

3. Share what friendship means to you.

4. Do you remember your very first friend? Explain.

5. How does a person make a friend?

WRITE A SHORT ESSAY on one of the topics or CHOOSE A QUOTE from the readings and relate it to your life. Cite an example.

TOPIC: _____ DATE: _____

Quote from Reading (pp. _____) _____

SELECTED QUOTATIONS ON FRIENDSHIP

>It's little things
>>one by one—
>sharing humor,
>>having fun,
>remembering,
>>out of sight
>the other one
>>with delight.
>Caring, sharing,
>>always true,
>that makes friends
>>like me and you.

The depth and beauty of the students' definitions of friendship speak of their sincerity and maturity in experiencing a rich relationship with a good friend. The requirement for a friendship cited by many is that we can be ourselves.

STUDENT DISCUSSION/ESSAY

Students chose a famous quotation on friendship to further elicit their feelings on thoughts of past masters: philosophers, statesmen, men of letters.

When individuals feel love, they want to tell the whole world. It is not surprising then that the following quotation was chosen by many.

I love you not for what you are, but for what I am when I am with you. —Anonymous

A young man of few words read his essay first. "When I'm with a close friend, I feel that I'm the happiest person in the world, and no one can pull me down...."

A young woman in love wrote: "Not only do I think of you as my boyfriend, but you are my best friend. I fear not to express to you both the pain and joy of my heart and mind. Emotions are brought to the surface...the hope and happiness I feel can be a part of me. I did not become the person I am because of you; but I am now the better person whom I have always wanted to be."

Another student who had experienced friendship wrote, "A good friend doesn't ask for the best in a person, but brings it out, and enhances the finest qualities that are within.

"A friend to me is you. You make my days brighter. You make me smile more, laugh more, and cry less. You help me to be me. Not only do I love you, but I respect and admire you. I want to help you be you. I wish I could give you half of all you've given to me. I wish I could be to someone what you have been to me. The best gift of my life is you." Her words were written from the heart, and read with feeling.

Friendship is a thing most necessary to life, since without friends no one would choose to live, though possessed of all advantages. —Aristotle

An insightful senior wrote: "No matter how great one's life is, no matter how rich or successful one might be, without having people to share it with, these things are nothing."

"Friends are the greatest things on earth. When you are feeling down and a friend calls or writes you a note just to say, 'I love you,' it makes all the difference in your mood. Friends make happiness. They bring smiles and good times. Without friends, what is there?" Kim smiled as she finished.

"My friends keep me going. Without them I would probably go crazy. I have friends to be there for me, and me for them. Without my friends I would not be able to express my emotions, and therefore, I would probably have problems that I could not handle...." This teen chose to write her feelings.

"My friends are so important to me. I can count on them. They make me feel so secure in just being myself...."

Greater love hath no man than this, that a man lay down his life for his friend. —John 15:13

From one young man: "My friend loves me so much that he was willing to give up some money that he put aside to take out his girl friend. His girl was very upset, because she was looking forward to going out to eat. But my friend faced that because he knew that he was my last hope."

Another wrote: "I believe that friends should help each other out no matter what, as long as it is not an illegal act. The joy you find with friends would be hard to replace. I believe that any human being should help out someone who is in need. Usually asking is the hardest thing, and helping is the easiest, because most friends are willing to give advice and to help."

One friend in a lifetime is much, two are many, three are hardly possible... —Henry Brooks Adams

"My one friend will almost assuredly last a lifetime. Right now, I have three excellent friends. I am not sure what they foresee in their future, but I am sure most of us will go our separate ways. The one friend for a lifetime is the one that I can tell all of my problems to without worry of his telling the whole damn world; a friend...will pick me up when I am down, and give me confidence in myself. A friend is one who will always be there through the good and the bad times."

Another student wrote: "I have found that there is the possibility of having more than two friends. If someone has a certain group of people they can turn to, then these are true friends."

A young woman's essay was a contradiction to this. She told of writing to a favorite aunt who lived out of town, expounding on the many friends in her crowd. "I remember my aunt's reply that a lifetime will show that though you may have many acquaintances, true friends can be counted on a few fingers."

The essence of friendship is entireness, a total magnanimity and trust. —Ralph Waldo Emerson

Magnanimity is defined by Webster as "generous to overlooking injury and insult." One student had cited in an earlier essay the importance of overlooking flaws in ourselves, and the need to overlook flaws in one's friends as well. Webster's definition, however, is more stringent. Overlooking injury and insult implies "forgiving those who trespass against us."

A male student wrote, "Friendship is important to me in relation to trust. A true friend is one you can trust and depend on, knowing that that friend will always be there for you, to help you with whatever. If you can't trust a good friend, whom can you trust?

"...without trust a friendship can exist, but it probably won't be a lasting one. To trust someone is to be able to leave them alone with your girlfriend and know they won't betray your trust."

Another young man chose his own quotation. He wrote: "I was reading about Francis Bacon, and I liked this quote: 'There is little friendship in this world, and least of all among equals.' I find this to be true when I look at my friends. They are all unique, but I chose them all for different reasons. They help me or I help them. It would be hard to be very close with someone with whom you are competing. I am very proud of the friends I have chosen."

A young woman wrote the following quotation in her journal: "Friendship is the inexpressible comfort of feeling safe with a person having neither to weigh thoughts nor measure words." —George Eliot

The anxiety of some people to make new friends is so intense that they never have old ones. —Anonymous

"This quote reminded me of another quote: 'Make new friends but keep the old.' I have a friend whom I have known since we were five years old. I used to live next door to her grandparents. When they both died her dad and stepmother moved into the house. We walked to and from grade school together. We both went our separate ways as teenagers in different high schools. I hope she will never forget the times we spent together. I know that I will not forget." This teen remembered an old and dear friend.

Wisdom is expressed by the student who wrote, "This quote is something to think about, because some people do give up their friends quickly. Some people keep switching groups, finding new friends. Others are so concerned about having many friends that they unconsciously ignore old friends."

A short but interesting comment from another student followed: "Some people cannot handle change, or learn to leave the past behind and start over. Other people cannot stay long enough to have the feeling of friendship."

There can be no friendship where there is not freedom. —William Penn

"Friends need space like any living thing. You have to let a friendship grow to become stronger, and that means giving the friends the freedom to be who they want to be." The young man agreed with Penn, and his words were direct.

Another student disagreed vehemently with Penn's statement. He wrote: "False. People who were slaves had friends. And people in jail have no freedom, but they still have friends."

Finally, in a poignant essay a young man tells of finding his friends. "While I was in the hospital for surgery, I learned a lot about my self-image, my friends and my family. My family and my best friends were by my side all the way. They showed their love for me in many ways. I felt so good just being around them. I am a happier and more positive person now, because I feel so loved. I thank God for my family and my friends. They were the ones who pulled me through. The surgery and the recovery were two of the best things that have happened in my life."

And in Anne's journal was a compelling essay. "Everyone can have a loving relationship, if they are willing to work at it. People cannot expect to be loved, if they never show love back, or show any kind of reaction to being loved. A person must care, share, help, be considerate, responsible, and honest. These all come out of loving. Also, one must never give up on someone who appears not to need love. A friend has to be there to give it."

Objective: To share personal interpretations of famous quotations on friendship

EXERCISE/JOURNAL SHEET

SELECTED QUOTATIONS ON FRIENDSHIP

Quotations from *On Friendship, a Selection,* edited by Louise Bachelder.

Comment on the following:

1. I love you not for what you are, but for what I am when I am with you. —Anonymous

2. Friendship is a thing most necessary to life, since without friends no one would choose to live, though possessed of all advantages. —Aristotle

3. Greater love hath no man than this, that a man lay down his life for his friend. —John 15:13

4. One friend in a lifetime is much; two are many; three are hardly possible...
   —Henry Brooks Adams

5. The essence of friendship is entireness, a total magnanimity and trust.
   —Ralph Waldo Emerson

6. The anxiety of some people to make new friends is so intense that they never have old ones. —Anonymous

7. There can be no friendship where there is not freedom. —William Penn

WRITE A SHORT ESSAY on one of the topics or CHOOSE A QUOTE from the readings. Relate it to yourself. Cite an example.

TOPIC: _____ DATE: _____

Quote from Reading (pp._____) _____

8   PEER PRESSURE

OBJECTIVES:

1. To recognize that peer pressure exists
2. To discuss areas governed by teenage peer pressure
3. To identify positive peer pressure
4. To recognize peer pressure to conform is powerful
5. To discuss feelings and concerns about alcohol and drugs
6. To know the law about and consequences of teen use of alcohol and drugs

AREAS OF PEER PRESSURE

Why is peer pressure so powerful? Each of us at sometime has fallen prey to peer pressure. It can bait us into compromising behavior. Excerpts from essays of students who preferred to pass in the discussions of loneliness and friendship attest to the vulnerability of some teenagers.

> "A friend is like a gift to have so you can share your life or feelings. There are good friends and bad friends. But it is better to have bad friends than no friends."

> "Without friends and the feeling of being wanted, you have little confidence and may not adapt to the school community."

> "Friends are special. When you spend a lot of time with a friend you tend to start to act like that person. You pick up their habits and start applying them to yourself."

> "In today's society, you have to do things you don't want to do, in order to survive. We all try to get into a crowd, and go along with the group. I know I do."

Acceptance by one's peers is a universal desire, a fact that has been true with each generation. Historically, peer pressure has written the laws of mankind that permit people to live in society. Nations have been able to function and grow. Institutions, large and small, have developed rules of procedure and of conduct. Even a well-run household has its set of rules that provides for harmony by designating responsibilities and setting limits, such as curfew.

Peer pressure relates to every identity. It can be positive and in our best interest. It can be harmful. Teenagers are the focus of much peer pressure. During teenage years acceptance by our peers is most important. To be accepted is to become a part of the social scene. For many, being identified as a member of a crowd equates with friendship. Although being part of a crowd requires conformity, it also offers opportunities for social activities, such as parties, as well as a place to hang out.

STUDENT DISCUSSION/ESSAY

Students are quick to respond to the areas governed by peer pressure:
- dress, hairstyle, make-up
- attitude, homework, risk taking
- alcohol, drugs, sex

A debonair young man opened the discussion. "I believe that peer pressure controls every aspect of a teenager's life. When we dress, we would never wear any of our clothes that were out of style, because we would be subject to ridicule. We might try out a new hairstyle, but nothing that is so radical that it would turn into the joke-of-the-day. The way we style our hair differs, but medium is the current style. Sex is definitely subject to peer pressure. In our group of guys, we always get excited when one of us has a successful weekend."

A more serious young man spoke up. "I feel that we all feel pressured to conform. Most of us do not want to stick out in a crowd or be a rebel. That's why we dress in similar clothes, and do many of the same things. We try to be like everyone else. I remember shopping for a new tie. I looked at the racks of stand-out-in-the-crowd ties. I remember thinking, 'I'll never wear one of those.' Later, I bought one, but I still haven't worn it."

"I, also, feel pressure to conform in terms of how I dress," said Lisa. "My parents give me their opinion, and my friends impose their style on me. I usually buy something that doesn't please me."

Then an assertive fellow spoke up. "I feel pressure to conform in a different area. I am an atheist, by choice, and it is incredible how many people try to convince me how wrong I am. I don't interfere in their lives, so who gave them the right to interfere in mine?"

"Peer pressure is related to our identity at a given time and place," offered a discerning young man. "As a son, there is peer pressure when I am out with a group of friends, as to whether I should obey my parents and go home on time. I feel ridiculous, but if I'm late I won't get the car next time. As a student, there is pressure to go out and have a good time, instead of doing my homework. There is also the concern of being considered a nerd that can pressure me. As an employee there is the pressure to agree with my boss, when I usually don't. There is also pressure to be patient with the elderly, when sometimes they are not patient with me."

Ed volunteered: "I've found that peer pressure can be positive. Freshman year, most of my friends were on the football team. After the season, they began to lift weights. I decided to go along and pump iron. I found that I had a fairly high tolerance for pain, and that I liked to compete. This led me to join the track team, and the next year to play football. These two sports have given to me a personal satisfaction in winning and competing. I also found new friends who had a will to succeed as I do."

"Same for me," put in Luke. "Football has become a great part of my life. Through football and the discipline involved, I have been able to discipline my life."

Joyce joined in: "When my girlfriend's parents were out of town, she stayed with me. She studied for hours, and she pressured me to turn off the TV and study with her. Now I feel guilty if I don't do my homework before I watch TV."

"I've known positive peer pressure, too," added Ryan. "On retreat, I admitted having a poor relationship with my mom. The guys convinced me to face my problem and talk to her. It would have been easy for them to tell me to forget her, but they gave me feedback in my best interest."

Objectives: *To recognize that peer pressure exists* EXERCISE/JOURNAL SHEET
To discuss areas of teenage peer pressure
To identify positive peer pressure

AREAS OF PEER PRESSURE

1. Circle areas governed by peer pressure.

   a. Dress   e. Diet   h. Hanging out

   b. Hairstyle   f. Alcohol   i. Sex

   c. Make-up   g. Drugs   j. Attitude

   d. Homework   k. Music

   Other _____ _____ _____

2. List peer pressure related to specific identities.

   a. As a son/daughter

   b. As a student

   c. As a teenager

   d. As an employee

3. Cite an example of positive peer pressure.

4. Why is it important to be accepted by your peers?

WRITE A SHORT ESSAY on one of the topics or CHOOSE A QUOTE from the readings. Relate it to yourself/someone you know. Cite an example. Include effect on you and on others.

TOPIC: _____ DATE: _____

Quote from Reading (pp._____) _____

THE HARMFUL INFLUENCE OF PEER PRESSURE

"As a teenager…
many of us wear masks to fit in.
If we are not considered one of the group—
regardless of whether or not we would want to be—
we are made to feel worthless.
I used to conform, but I got sick of not being myself."

DO YOU EVER FEEL PRESSURED TO CONFORM?

As a teenager there is the great desire to be accepted, to be popular and fun to be with. Some of us search for a crowd that will accept us socially. The business of the crowd is to be "cool." To be "cool" implies to drink at weekend parties. For some crowds the pressure to conform is extended to include experimenting with drugs and being sexually active. For others to be "cool" means to fit a prescribed pattern of dress and action, fast driving, easy money, defying parents, and taking risks with alcohol and drugs. These are considered exciting as long as "parents don't know."

STUDENT DISCUSSION/ESSAY

"If you want to be a member of the crowd you have to go along with the group. Yeah, I have felt pressure to conform. I've done things that I would not do if I were alone. I think everybody does it to show off or just to get along with the others. We should just be ourselves in the things that we do, and think more about it before we do it," admitted a thoughtful young man.

"I feel pressure to conform in school when I am with certain popular friends," said Amy. "I find myself not acting as I normally would, but as I think they want me to. Just recently, I have realized that being myself is more exciting than imitating them."

"There is pressure among my friends in terms of drinking and using drugs on the weekend at parties," confessed another in his essay. "But a moral accepted among my friends is not to drink and drive… I say no to anything that is immoral. I have smoked wood, and I have tried alcohol, but I have chosen not to use them. Most of the time I am the designated driver. They seem to respect me because they let me hang around, and they still talk to me."

DOES PEER PRESSURE INFLUENCE YOUR ACTIONS IN TERMS OF TRYING DRUGS AND ALCOHOL?

Is the "everyone is doing it" syndrome the rationale used by the crowd to influence us to experiment with alcohol and/or drug use? Is it an ego or a power trip that fuels the leader(s) of a given crowd to entice others into rebellious behavior?

STUDENT DISCUSSION/ESSAY

A redhead spoke up boldly: "I do not feel peer pressure influences many people. The way I see it, those who want to drink and do drugs choose it on their own. Those who don't want to use them are not disliked because of their decision. Often they are respected for it."

"I feel peer pressure definitely plays a part!" Joel insisted. "I have chosen not to drink alcohol, because I feel no need to, and that it is bad for me. I worry that it might hurt my performance in school, sports, at work, and in my relationships with others. None of my really good friends drink, so there isn't a lot of pressure except from those in a crowd who feel that I want to be accepted by them.

"I've never felt pressure to conform, but I've seen others do it. A guy I know started smoking when he changed friends. He didn't smoke before that, but being with new peers, he changed. He looks happy, though, being with them."

"I never felt pressured to experiment with illegal drugs, but sometimes I feel pressure to use alcohol," admitted another.

"Drinking is something that I haven't tried yet, either. To admit this, it seems like I'm the only one who has fallen through the cracks of experimenting. I do think that drinking is different from smoking and using drugs. I used to be against drinking, but peer pressure changed the way I feel about it. I see that my friends always have someone to watch over them when they drink. A designated driver would make sure that everyone gets home safely. The only people who are affected by alcohol are those who choose to drink it. So I figure that drinking is all right since no one gets hurt," was Allen's opinion.

"How can you say that?" Karen blurted out. "What about the effect on those who do drink? Do you think it won't harm them?"

"Karen's right. Most teens can't handle alcohol," said Craig. "I had a friend who went to a new school where he started to drink to be accepted by a crowd. He wanted new friends. I told him that it wasn't worth it, that they are not true friends if they expect you to drink. He told me that he could handle it. Within a couple of months, he wanted to drink every night. I told him that he needed to get help. Then he told me that I wasn't a good friend. Now he's an alcoholic, and he won't get help."

"Let's be honest. Alcohol can be addictive, and alcohol is connected with peer pressure." A mature young man addressed the issue. "I know kids who feel if their buddies are drinking then they should be also, or they will be ridiculed. Most people just want to fit into the 'in' crowd even though they know what they are doing is wrong!

"If friends tell you to have a beer, it's your choice whether you have one or not. If you decline, your true friends will still see you as the same person. Just because you don't drink doesn't mean you're a wimp. It just means that you don't drink. If you do drink, you don't drive!

"I wish I could have a beer once in a while with my friends, but it tastes awful and I wouldn't normally drink something that tastes as bad as beer, so I won't drink." His statement was honest, but it sounded more like a lament than anything else.

DO MOST TEENAGERS DRINK?

There are some of us who like to control people. Some of us like to follow others. There are those of us who remain in control of ourselves—immune to the pressures of our peers. It is always a matter of choice.

Claire Safran, in her article "Let's Get Wasted," writes that the most common reason teens start drinking is peer pressure. She reports that alcohol abuse far exceeds drug abuse, and that with the increase in alcohol abuse among teenagers comes the escalation in teenage problem drinkers, and the rise in yearly teen fatalities linked to alcohol use.

STUDENT DISCUSSION/ESSAY

"'I'm sick of school. I just can't wait until this weekend so I can get drunk.' This is what I commonly hear in the lunch room every day," revealed David. "It seems as if some kids don't have anything else to live for. They get drunk with their buddies Friday or Saturday night, or both."

"I've noticed peers who drink to be cool. They get a buzz on before football or basketball games. They talk loud and have their own private jokes. I wouldn't want to get started on it. It's not cool; it just slowly makes you stupid." Some are willing to speak up about this common teenage pastime.

"Hey, I enjoy drinking on weekends and before a game. I always have a sober driver, too. But I laugh when potheads say that alcohol is worse than pot for the body. Alcohol wears off over time. Pot screws up your head forever!"

"I don't feel that just because you have a designated driver it's okay to drink!" announced Stacy. "Drinking is wrong. It's illegal for kids our age to buy alcohol in our state. Yet teenagers find it easy to get."

A serious teen wrote: "I feel that there are only a few teenagers who do not or never have drunk alcohol. These few may choose not to drink for a number of reasons:
1) an alcoholic family member
2) strong moral values
3) influence of others (parents, friends, etc.)
4) a strong sense of individuality
5) enough self-confidence to stand up for what they believe.

Whatever reason a non-drinker has, he or she always has the respect of his or her peers. Non-drinkers will get more respect for standing up for their convictions than by going along with the crowd."

Objective: *To recognize that peer pressure to conform is powerful* EXERCISE/JOURNAL SHEET

THE HARMFUL INFLUENCE OF PEER PRESSURE

Comment on the following:

1. Do you ever feel pressured to conform? Explain.

2. Does peer pressure influence your actions in terms of trying drugs and alcohol? How? Why?

3. Do most teenagers drink?

WRITE A SHORT ESSAY on one of the topics or CHOOSE A QUOTE from the readings. Cite an example. Relate it to self/someone you know. Include the effect on you/others.

TOPIC: _____ DATE: _____

Quote from Reading (pp._____) _____

THE HARMFUL EFFECTS OF DRUGS AND ALCOHOL

There is a rippling effect
from those who use drugs and alcohol that
touches many lives.

HAVE YOU EVER KNOWN ANYONE WHOSE LIFE WAS CONTROLLED BY DRUGS OR ALCOHOL?

Students who remained silent during most of the earlier discussion chose to comment on this question.

STUDENT DISCUSSION/ESSAY

"I think that excessive drinking is very wrong. My uncle drank a lot, and it hurt his family emotionally, and hurt his health," related a resolute young teen.

"My sister had a problem with drinking. She used to get drunk every weekend," admitted Lori. "Her drinking had a bad effect on our family. At dinner time, everyone was silent. My dad never had the same amount of trust in her or me, even though I never drank and still don't. My sister has quit drinking completely, and our lives are pretty much back to normal, but not all the way."

Another young woman spoke up. "I have seen drinking change a person's personality. People can become mean or cruel, and sometimes act violently. Other times they act stupidly, or become forgetful. I think that teenagers drink hoping to have fun, or to go along with the crowd. But drinking can hurt people in many different ways, both emotionally and physically." Her eyes had been witness to scenes she would rather forget.

Eager to be next, Andrea spoke soberly: "Yes, drinking can have a tremendous effect on a person's life. My friend's sister was driving home from her job one night, just two days before Christmas, when she was hit by a car driven by a drunk driver and killed instantly."

A silence followed, and in a quiet voice Jolene spoke: "My dad was cited for drunk driving. He had been at a party with his friends, a quarter of a mile from our house. On his way home, he drove off the road and hit a light pole. He said that he had twelve beers—and seven 'jays'?" Someone suggested the word *pot*. "Thanks. That's right, pot. The police cited him, and he had to go to jail for about a month. Now he goes to AA meetings. If some of you underage boozers get caught, the court won't show you any mercy, either." She added, "I keep trying to understand why so many teenagers want to experiment with their lives."

"Hey, drinking and abusing alcohol are two different things. There is no problem if you drink, get drunk and wake up with a hangover. There is a problem if you get drunk, and do something destructive like trashing the house where the party is held, or fighting, or even worse, driving," Jason spoke out boldly.

"If my brother's drinking ever hurt anyone, it had to be my mother. He would say hurtful things to her. Mom was just heartsick when he came home drunk," Teri admitted.

WHAT ABOUT TEENAGERS' USE OF DRUGS?

A national survey conducted by Substance Abuse and Mental Health Services Administration reports, "Drug abuse is a plague that continues to tear American communities apart. It is linked to crime, AIDS, and family violence.... Eight out of ten adult drug users started as teens; half started at age sixteen or younger" (National Household Survey on Drug Abuse, 1991).

STUDENT DISCUSSION/ESSAY

"Drugs are out there, and kids are going to get involved. A lot of teenagers try drugs out of curiosity. Everyone wants to see what they're like. It's going to take a lot to stop kids using them, but I'm sure we can, if we try." This young woman was upbeat and optimistic.

"If I didn't smoke pot with this guy, then I wasn't his friend; I just couldn't be part of his group anymore. Pot fixed him up bad."

In an unsigned essay, a boy wrote: "Drugs are a major part of my life. It started with marijuana; then I needed crack and CP to get high. I have tried cocaine, but do not like the effects. I will occasionally sell drugs in Cleveland. This is a scary business. There are dope men after me every time I sell. I have been involved in shootings, and it is only a matter of time before the cops get me, or I get shot. The money is good, and the drugs are good. I love everything about drugs. I know I need help, but I can't ask for it."

Another young man wrote: "I was at my friend's house watching a movie about a poor woman who spent all of her money on drugs. When she came home high, she would hit her children and trash the house. During this movie my friend told me his older brother acted like that. He would come home after a wild party and beat him. He showed me some of his scars. I was shocked. I decided that I would promise myself never to do any drugs. I thought how that would make me feel, having my brother come home and beat me.... It does not matter what party or social event I go to, there will always be people there doing drugs. My only words for those people are, 'I don't need that stuff. So, keep it away from me.'"

HAVE YOU EVER TRIED TO HELP SOMEONE WITH A DRINKING/DRUG PROBLEM?

It is often difficult to stand up for what we believe. There is always the risk of losing a friendship. Also, saying no to alcohol or to drugs in a group of peers may be a risk in terms of acceptance by the group. There is always a choice—a personal choice. Life is always challenging us.

STUDENT DISCUSSION/ESSAY

"A few months ago at a party, a classmate of mine, who had been drinking a lot, was in his car ready to pull out," Sue recounted. "I went up to the car and tried to persuade him not to drive. I was able to get his car keys. He yelled at me, and made a huge scene. I felt awkward, but I knew that I was doing the right thing. Other people helped me. We drove him and his car home safely. I felt good about the situation, even though it ruined my friendship with him."

"Something similar happened to me at a party last summer," Bob recalled. "I was just having a good time socializing when I noticed this person, whom I had always looked up to, drinking. After watching him down several beers, it seemed to me that he was overdoing it. The thing that bothered me was that he was an athlete. I didn't want to see alcohol take control of his life. I tried to convince him to seek help. He avoided me for a long time. He saw my concern as an intrusion on his private life. Sometime later, he did get help. Today, he is speaking to me again."

HAVE YOU EVER JUST SAID NO? WHAT WAS THE EFFECT ON YOU AND YOUR RELATIONSHIP WITH THE GROUP?

Peer pressure exists as a part of our daily lives, and this has been true in all countries through all generations. Peer pressure is one way that life questions us. By our choices, we determine how we are going to live our lives. On a larger scale, individual choices help to determine our accountability to our civilization. Today issues such as human rights, the environment, and abortion, plus the health hazards of using drugs, alcohol, and tobacco are the personal and global concerns impacting young people as much as adults.

STUDENT DISCUSSION/ESSAY

"My first weekend party was a real experience," Tim admitted. "There were many kids smoking drugs. One person who was high came over and asked me if I wanted to try it. I refused. When he insisted, I told him that I felt fine. I didn't want a drug to take me to fantasy land. Finally, he went away to bother some other kid. This incident did not affect my relationship with the group. Some respected me for saying no. I was glad that they still liked me."

Tim joined in the discussion: "At a party, when I was offered a beer and declined, they accepted my decision. This helped me. I thought that at parties I would be pressured to drink. Later in the basement I saw this kid on the couch throw up. They said that he drank a lot and was a lightweight. A friend made sure that he did not choke. It made me glad that I didn't drink."

A shy young woman took her turn. "I have a really close friend who has seriously impressed me with her actions. She has been in some situations where she was faced with peer pressure to try sex, drugs, and alcohol. She stood up to them, keeping her morals, even though it cost her a friendship. I really hope that in a similar situation I can keep mine."

Bradley was next to speak. "My brother has been involved in alcohol and drug use for many years. His experience was an important influence on my decision not to use either. My brother is twenty-three years old. He started drinking in junior high and got into pot in high school. His friends had a great influence on him. He got into trouble at school, and dropped out in the tenth grade. Everyone else in the family has gone to college. He could have, too. But now he has no diploma, a difficult menial job, and a heavy addiction to support."

A lanky, soft-spoken young man added: "Peer pressure doesn't influence me. I could care less whether or not people want me to use drugs or alcohol. I'll use them or not use them, as I choose. Nothing angers me more than people stepping into my life. If others want to do that sort of thing, fine. I may not agree with it, but I realize I can't do anything about it. To each his own, including myself."

Another wrote: "Just like any other human being, I have a yearning to be accepted. I like to be liked. Sometimes, I think this characteristic hurts me because I conform to what people want me to be, and not what I really am...I worry about what other people think of me...I guess that it is the fear of rejection that causes me to hide my real self."

Objective: To discuss feelings and concerns about alcohol and drugs   EXERCISE/JOURNAL SHEET

THE HARMFUL EFFECT OF DRUGS AND ALCOHOL

1. Have you ever known anyone (youth or adult) whose life was controlled by drugs and/or alcohol?

2. What about teenagers' use of drugs?

3. Have you ever tried to help someone with a drinking or drug problem? Explain.

4. Have you ever said no to risk-taking behavior? What was the effect on you and your relationship with the group?

WRITE A SHORT ESSAY on one of the topics CHOOSE A QUOTE from the readings. Cite an example. Relate it to self/someone you know. Include effect on you/others.

TOPIC: _____ DATE: _____

Quote from Reading (pp._____) _____

Objective: To find out the law and the consequences for getting arrested for alcohol   PROJECT SHEET

KNOW THE LAW AND THE CONSEQUENCES FOR USING ALCOHOL

Since laws pertaining to alcohol and drug use vary from state to state, and from municipality to municipality, it is important to learn the local and state laws, and the penalties relating to them. Know your rights and responsibilities under our legal system.

Invite a local law enforcement professional or a person from juvenile court to your class to address the following questions related to teenage use of alcohol, and those on the next sheet relating to teen drug use.

1. What is the legal age to purchase alcohol?

2. What are the current local laws related to teenage drinking?

3. Can parents be held liable for teenage drinking? Under what circumstances is this true?

4. What are the penalties under the law for persons prosecuted for teenage drinking?

5. What action is taken if a juvenile is cited for drunk driving?

6. What are the penalties for drunk driving by an adult?

7. Can a person be arrested for buying alcohol for teenagers? If so, what is the penalty?

8. How are the laws pertaining to teenage drinking enforced locally?

9. Can a person be arrested for serving alcohol to a minor? Is the person who serves the drink or the establishment held accountable? What are the consequences?

10. Where do most teenagers get their alcohol?

Objective: To know the law and consequences for getting arrested for teen drug use   PROJECT SHEET

GETTING BUSTED FOR DRUGS *

1. What are the current laws regarding illegal drug use?

2. How are these laws enforced in your locality?

3. What are the penalties for breaking these laws?

4. What is the potential for getting arrested?

5. If arrested, what is likely to happen? Is going to jail or to reform school possible?

6. How are the laws and penalties applied to juveniles as opposed to adults?

7. Under the law, what constitutes a "juvenile"?

8. What happens in juvenile court? Do juveniles need lawyers?

9. Can juveniles have lawyers?

10. Do adolescents have any legal rights? What, if any, are they?

11. Can adolescents be processed through the adult criminal courts?

12. What goes on in adult courts?

13. Where does someone turn for help? What alternatives are there?

14. What if someone cannot afford a lawyer?

* Jim Inciardi (Beschner, 1986).

9 HUMAN SEXUALITY

OBJECTIVES:

1. To think ahead about my decision about having sex
2. To affirm that having sex is a choice
3. To recognize the serious risks involved in having sex
4. To learn the facts about STDs and HIV
5. To recognize the risks of pregnancy and teen parenting
6. To plan ahead for my life

FOCUS ON HUMAN SEXUALITY

"Sex in teenage years is increasingly common.... Today, 56% of women and 73% of men have had intercourse before their 18th birthday" (Guttmacher Institute, 1994). "It is estimated that 1,000,000 teenage girls between the ages of 15 and 19 become pregnant each year in the United States. The ratio of approximately 1 out of 10 has changed very little since 1973. These girls represent all social, economic and racial backgrounds, rich and poor. There is no common denominator" (Gore, 1990). "Of the 1 million teenage women who become pregnant every year, the vast majority are unintentional. About half of adolescent pregnancies end in birth" (Guttmacher Institute, 1994).

STUDENT DISCUSSION/ESSAY

Rachel, a young social worker, volunteered to speak on the subject of human sexuality. Dressed in faded jeans, a sweat shirt, and jogging shoes, she perched on the edge of the desk. Slowly, she looked at each student, gave a flip to her short blonde hair, and with a dimpled smile said, "Hi! I'm the middle child in a family of seven children and one of four girls. You can ask me anything about life, and I will not be surprised. (She often paused as she spoke.) I remember my mother as always being pregnant, and she was always tired. We wore hand-me-down clothes. My father was an alcoholic and rarely home. We knew nothing about "quality time" with a parent. My mother was busy just trying to keep everything together. I had nobody to talk to. I was different from my sisters. I was more of a rebel. So at eighteen and a high school graduate, I decided to take control of my life. I got a job, found a place to live, and moved out on my own. It was a big responsibility, but I was old enough to make my own decisions. What I did with my life was up to me."

She tossed out a few questions. "How many of you have a job? That's it, a show of hands. Good. How many of you have a savings account? a driver's license? a checking account? Each of these is a privilege, and with each comes rights and responsibilities.

"Today our focus is on human sexuality. Traditionally, there are moral constraints. Always, there are grave responsibilities: the risk of AIDS, STDs (sexually transmitted diseases), and pregnancy. A person does not choose his or her sexual orientation, but a person does make a choice in terms of having a sexual relationship.

"You may not be contemplating marriage, but some of you may be contemplating relationships. I want you to consider what decisions you will make and what your responsibilities will be. When it comes to a decision about having sex, you can't remain indifferent. Make your decision early within yourself; decide to stick with it. There is a lot of pressure on young people from the media. Sex sells everything. They want you to think that sex is everything, that sex is free. Sex is not free. Sex is a choice. Think about it. Think about what you want to do with your life. This is serious.

"Once one of you young women has a physical relationship with a young man everything changes. A reputation takes years to build, and only one night to destroy. Some girls want to be popular. Well, if you say yes, he will get the word around the next day! When a young man makes a score with a young woman, she becomes locker room talk.

"If you respect yourself, your choice is moral. It's easiest to make your choice early. Make it now, and stick with it. It's your life. Don't put yourself in a position of having to save yourself or give yourself away! This is vital to your future. If you sleep with someone, and they have slept with someone, who slept with someone else, you have slept with them all as far as sexually infectious disease is concerned. You can't remain indifferent. Decide now to say no and avoid many problems.

"Young women must recognize that a man pushed to the extreme will be forceful. Men are physical and can't be separated from it. Don't tease them. This is not a game. If you decide not to have sex, then don't send mixed messages. Don't act in a seductive way.

"A woman needs caring and tenderness. There is a difference between sex and love making. If you say no to sex, explain why, and he will respect you. If he can't respect your decision, he can't respect you.

"Can you talk to your parents? Where do values come from? What has happened to you in your lifetime? How well do you know yourself? When does life begin?"

She didn't answer the questions. She paused and then continued: "What experiences will you take out of your family background? My parents did a lot of yelling. When I got married at nineteen, my husband told me that I did a lot of yelling! What cycles do you want to break? You are an adult. It's your choice. After I thought about it, I quit yelling. I didn't want that as a part of my life."

Someone asked about premarital sex. She answered, "Are you going to ask someone to have an AIDS test? So many things are going around now. The other day, I asked a teenager how she felt about her pregnant sister. She responded, 'I can't stand it!'

"Premarital sex confuses many issues. Love is possessive. Are you ready to give up your independence to choose your way of life? Are you ready for the responsibilities which may be the consequence of your actions?

"Some use sex as punishment." Rachel continued in a very dramatic voice: "You may think, 'my family doesn't give me any love, so I'm going to get it elsewhere.' It doesn't work that way. Boys want to know you. Know what they can get.

"What about safe sex? They are giving condoms away in some schools. Does that mean that sex is safe? How safe is safe? Is 85 to 90 percent safe, safe? What if you are the one in ten? Avoid situations when you might be tempted to go farther sexually that you really want to—like private time alone making out together. Be really safe; stay with a group. Do fun things with others—go to a movie, go bowling, volunteer to work together with the stage crew for the musical. Talk to each other; get to know each other; learn to respect each other.

"I was married at nineteen. We had a child. We came close to divorce. It's been a hard road, but I went back to school. Finally, I have an identity. We are a family. I am here to tell you that life gets better. Don't blow it. Life gets better!"

Objective: To discuss the importance of thinking ahead
about my decision regarding a sexual relationship

EXERCISE/JOURNAL SHEET

FOCUS ON HUMAN SEXUALITY

Comment on the following:

1. Write three statements made by the social worker that impressed you. Why?

    a.

    b.

    c.

2. When it comes to a decision about having sex, why is it important to think ahead?

3. What actions can you take that will help you to stick to your decision to say no to sex?

WRITE A SHORT ESSAY on one of the topics above. Cite an example. Relate it to yourself or to someone you know. Include the effect on the person.

TOPIC: _____ DATE: _____

HUMAN SEXUALITY: CONSIDER THE CONSEQUENCES

> "Sex education should be about nothing less than
> how and when
> we have loved and trusted and believed
> enough
> to hand over the astonishing gift of self."
> — Sharon A. Sheehan

A MATTER OF CHOICE

Our lives are governed by the choices that we make on a day-to-day basis. No decision has greater ramifications on a young person's life than the decision she or he will make in terms of having a sexual relationship.

Human sexuality is a matter of choice. There are many sexual influences preying on us as we grow from puberty into adulthood. The influences of peer pressure and the media are constant, but the physical risks of AIDS, STDs, and pregnancy are an ever-growing reality.

The consequences of having a sexual relationship are serious, and should be weighed carefully by an individual before making a decision.

"Every year three million teenagers acquire a sexually transmitted disease, which can imperil their ability to have children or lead to serious health problems, such as cancer and infection with the AIDS virus" (Guttmacher Institute, 1994).

AIDS is an epidemic. Everyone who engages in promiscuous sexual relations is at risk. The human immunodeficiency virus (HIV) that causes AIDS is transmitted by sexual intercourse (as well as in other ways, such as sharing of needles by drug users). There are many other serious sexually transmitted diseases in addition to AIDS, such as chlamydia, herpes simplex virus (HSV), condyloma (genital warts), syphilis, gonorrhea, chancroid tumors, and hepatitis B virus. Each of these can have lasting, life-long consequences, and many are transmitted not only by sexual intercourse but also through apparently innocuous or even unknown rashes or other breaks in the skin.

"More than 13 million STD infections occur each year. Because many females have no obvious symptoms, they often go undiagnosed. As a result, these women are more likely to suffer such complications as pelvic inflammatory disease, infertility, and ectopic pregnancy in adulthood" (Leslie Laurence).

"The only safe sex is no sex."

The moral restraints that once were the norm, and heeded in our culture, remain. There is within each of us a consciousness of right and wrong. For those who take pride in themselves and have strong family values, choices will be moral ones.

STUDENT DISCUSSION/ESSAY

A young man spoke with conviction to open a discussion: "How can a person not be intimidated by the thought that sex is everything? In the movies and on television, sex is portrayed as the end all. It is used so much in advertising. But sex is only seen as sex; not as an act of love. The media has control over what kids think: 'If actors engage in sex, it must be OK.' The catch is that they never show the consequences. A person could get AIDS, become pregnant or contact a sexually transmitted disease!"

"Right!" Leo agreed. "Teens have to think about the consequences of sex before they jump in the sack. Most teens know about AIDS and pregnancy being a risk, but they think a condom will protect them. I think that teens would hesitate a little more if they realized that there are sexual diseases that a condom won't protect them from."

Marc added: "Yes, and teens also need to think about their relationship with another person. They often fall head over heels in love, and think that they will never love anyone else. So, hey! Why not hit the sack? They will be married as soon as they graduate from high school anyway. Or will they? Some people marry their teenage heart throb, but how many? Most likely they will break up for some stupid reason, and then fall head over heels in love with someone else."

"What happens when a couple breaks up right after they do the posturepedic polka? One of them spreads rumors, some of which are true, about their little experience. You know what happens? They are the topic of the day!" Chuckles were heard as he finished speaking.

Leo pulled them back to being serious, saying: "We may be able to do whatever we want, so long as our parents don't know, but once we think about it, we may not want to."

Hallie held up a newspaper clipping, and waved it to be recognized. "I cut out an article from Ann Lander's column about a seventeen-year-old girl who lamented having allowed boys to have sex with her." She read it to the group:

"...A lot of girls use sex to keep a boy interested. Why do we do this when all our lives we are told by parents, church and school that it is wrong? I guess virginity seems old-fashioned in the '90s. But I've learned that some things never go out of style.

"In both of my relationships, I can look back and see that before sex entered the picture, we laughed more, talked more and went to a lot more places. Once you cross the line, it's all the guy wants to do.

"Boys don't respect girls who put out. If a guy decides to break up, it won't make any difference whether you've had sex or not. If you use sex to hold on to him, that will be the only part of you he's interested in."... (Signed) Feeling Used Again in Oregon (Ann Landers)

One young woman turned in her essay unsigned. "As a teenager, I don't feel that I am an expert on sex. My mom is aware that I don't view sex as only for marriage. Yet, I don't believe in casual sex. I am a senior, and I have had sex with only one person, and I truly love this person. I waited five months before we had sex, and there were times when I did doubt my feelings as well as his. What I did was against my religious beliefs, and yet I don't believe what I did was sinful. I learned a lot about life, love, and relationships. We grew together and taught each other. I believed in my decision, yet I do not want to have sex again until I am married. I did not make a mistake, but it's hard when you are young. I still have to find myself. I will never forget him. I would not have wanted it with anyone else. I will always love and respect him. I don't appreciate talking about it. I don't gossip about it. I am not seeing him, but we are best friends."

HAVE YOU WITNESSED THE REALITIES OF TEENAGE PREGNANCY AND TEENAGE PARENTING?

"Some teens think that they are too young to get pregnant. However, in industrialized countries, a girl's menstrual cycle may begin as early as age ten. The age of puberty has fallen dramatically" (Suzanne Wymelenberg).

A teenager's life opportunities are dramatically changed when a young woman becomes a teenage mother. In some cases the environment for the child is less than optimal.

STUDENT DISCUSSION/ESSAY

Excerpts from student essays reveal the realities of teenage pregnancy. "Just yesterday after school, a girl told my sister that she was pregnant. The school nurse gave her the test twice. It was positive. She is thirteen years old and in the eighth grade. The boy's condom broke."

Another wrote, "Many young teens are pressured or confused when other teens tell them that having sex at an early age is safe. A friend of mine is very depressed because her boyfriend broke up with her when she said no to sex. I know of many of my peers who were pressured into it."

Andrea spoke up: "My cousin was pregnant at sixteen. She put the baby up for adoption. Two years later she was pregnant again, and decided to keep her baby. She found that it wasn't like it is in the movies. She found herself asking family members for help and guidance. She lost trust from the family and her freedom. She wasn't financially fit to care for a baby. Now, three years later at twenty-one, she is still struggling. I don't think that I could do that because I'm not ready. I probably won't be until after college. I want to get my life organized before I organize someone else's."

"Let's face it, when it comes to sex the heavy responsibility is with the young woman! There is a double standard. If a girl gets pregnant, she not only carries the baby, but she carries the consequences! Men can walk away, and most of them do." Lori was pragmatic.

"Not necessarily," retorted Jim. "My best friend and his girlfriend have a son. My friend is taking responsibility of this child, and is helping to support it. They have accepted the consequences and seem to be happy. The baby is growing up in a good environment, and will probably be very healthy. This may have taken a lot away from their teenage lives, but they feel responsible for their actions."

This from an essay: "I have witnesses a girl become a teenage parent. It's horrible. She has so much resentment for the child. She blames the child for ruining her life. But the child didn't ruin her life; the teenagers did by not controlling their actions."

Another young teen wrote: "I knew a girl who had a great personality, was good looking, and was going far in life. She got pregnant in high school, which prevented her from going to college and getting a good job. The child's father cut out on her when he learned that she was pregnant. She has since married and had another child. I sometimes wonder, and I'll bet she does too, what she could have become."

THE CASE FOR CHASTITY

> Perhaps the best and most beautiful reason
> to choose chastity
> is one's faith commitment—
> one's love and respect for God,
> for one's self and
> for the other person.

"Despite the trends, teenagers generally do not initiate sexual intercourse as early as most adults believe. Nor do all teenagers have sex. Although the likelihood of having intercourse increases steadily with age, nearly 20% of adolescents do not have intercourse at all during their teenage years. Moreover, many of the youngest teenagers who have had intercourse report that they were forced to do so" (Guttmacher Institute, 1994).

The safety argument that stresses the use of contraceptives is a weak one. "One in four sexually active teens between 15 and 19 doesn't use a contraceptive. Each year, 2.5 million teenagers, one in six, are infected by a sexually transmitted disease. AIDS has killed 26,159 people in the past ten years; 196,000 currently have the disease. And 1.5 million more Americans are thought to be infected.... These statistics and an exclusive poll by *USA Weekend* show strong support for the chastity message (Kathleen McCleary).

There are many reasons to abstain. "It has been established in all major studies of marital adjustment that girls and boys who have been virgins before marriage make better adjustments in marriage and are less likely to divorce than those who have had premarital sex. According to psychiatrist Dr. David Mace, in *The New Sexuality,* the answer appears to be because they are people with ego-strength and conventional attitudes" (Eugene C. Kennedy).

Listing facts about abstinence, Richard P. Barth refers to statistics for teens in large cities as reported in 1987. "At age 15, about 82% of all girls have not had sex. About 40% of males and 60% of females under 17 report never having sex.... There are strong personal, medical and relationship-building reasons for teenagers not to have sex" (Richard Barth).

Many teenagers choose alcohol, drugs, and sex as symbols of adulthood. But the truer signs of maturity are a philosophy of life that makes values a part of their thinking, and a set of beliefs that will enable them to make intelligent choices.

In his book *How To Be An Adult,* David Richo defines *value* as esteeming the worth of something, declaring its meaning. He relates values to self-esteem, and reminds us that values arise from within and give us a sense of our own identity. We are what we value. Our choices reveal the who of our person. According to Richo, "Our personal values identify us to ourselves and others. In a very real way, we are the values we cherish and demonstrate."

Moral values reflect in all we say and do. They form our personality and affect our self-esteem. Moral values are the pride of loving parents. They are the measure of love and respect for family life. They are the fiber that makes us a people of strength and potential, and a nation of justice and goodwill.

Eugene Kennedy, writing in *The New Sexuality,* tells of young people's need of the "supportive presence of adults." He refers to people who believe in something and have had to work hard at understanding what they believe.

STUDENT DISCUSSION/ESSAY

Peg spoke up. "I'm disappointed in some of my friends who have 'given in.' I had kind of looked up to them for having so many dates. I thought they had never given in. That's being popular? That's their choice."

Lexie raised her hand to speak next, "I like the idea about persons making their choice early, within themselves, and sticking to it. Many of us have, many of us do, and with the media coverage stressing the spread of AIDS, more teenagers will decide to say no to sex."

"My choice is based on moral values. Values are a gift passed down through our families. Just as we are guided by laws, we need to be guided by tradition. Tradition unites people, and helps people keep in touch with their past in relation to their future. Our choices come easier when they are based on our values. At least, that's the way it is in my family," said Amy.

In her essay, Julianne, a mature young woman, wrote: "My father has an expression that gives assurance to each of us when we go for a job interview or such. He says, 'Remember, what you are speaks so loudly I can't hear a word you say.' I have cherished this thought. To me he was saying that the values we have clung to in the choices we have made are expressed in the uniqueness of our person."

Objective: To learn the facts about STDs and HIV   PROJECT SHEET

THE FACTS ABOUT STDs AND HIV*

Richard P. Barth defines STDs as a group of communicable diseases that are usually spread through sexual contact.... "About one in eight teenagers currently have an STD."

Invite a professional from your county Department of Health to your class to address the following questions:

1. For each of the following STDs, explain how it is acquired, how prevented, the symptoms, treatment, and the changes they can make in one's life.

    a. Syphilis

    b. Gonorrhea

    c. Herpes

    d. Chlamydia

2. What is HIV?

3. What is AIDS?

4. How is AIDS transmitted?

5. Name some ways HIV is *not* transmitted.

6. Who is at risk?

7. How can the risk of becoming HIV-infected be eliminated?

8. What is the HIV antibody test?

9. What are the symptoms of HIV infection?

10. How long can a person be infected with HIV before being diagnosed with AIDS?

11. Will everyone with HIV die?

12. Is there a vaccine, cure, or treatment?

13. How would HIV change my life?

*(Barth, 1993)

WRITE A SHORT ESSAY. Choose one of the STDs or HIV. How would having it change your life?

TOPIC: _____ DATE: _____

Objectives: To establish that sex is a choice
To recognize the possible consequences
of having a sexual relationship

EXERCISE/JOURNAL SHEET

HUMAN SEXUALITY: CONSIDER THE CONSEQUENCES

Comment on the following:

1. Who/what has the greatest influence on you in terms of not having sex? Explain.

2. Are you aware of the serious consequences in terms of personal physical risks involved in having a sexual relationship? Explain.

3. Have you witnessed a teenage pregnancy and the realities of it?

4. Make a case for chastity.

WRITE A SHORT ESSAY on one of the topics or CHOOSE A QUOTE from the readings. Cite an example. Relate it to self/another. Include the effect on you/others.

TOPIC: _____ DATE: _____

Quote from Reading (pp._____) _____

HUMAN SEXUALITY AND THE PROSPECT OF POVERTY

The "feminization of poverty" is a frightening phrase! But it is true. The cycle of poverty begins with an unintended teenage pregnancy.

"More than 80% of young women who give birth are from poor and low-income families. These young mothers tend not only to be disadvantaged economically, educationally and socially at the time of their child's birth, but also to be at risk of falling further behind their more advantaged peers who postponed childbearing to obtain more education and to advance their careers. Teenage mothers, for example, obtain less education and have lower future family incomes than young women who delay their first birth. Many are poor later in life, and while it is clear that their initial disadvantaged background is a major reason for their subsequent poverty, it is also clear that early childbearing has a lasting impact on the lives and future opportunities of young mothers and of their children" (Guttmacher Institute, 1994).

Most teenage mothers drop out of school. Of the teen mothers who bear a child before age eighteen, only 20% complete high school. Of teen mothers fifteen or younger only 10% will graduate from high school! Studies show that teenage marriages have a high rate of divorce. In addition almost half of the teen mothers are pregnant again within three years (Feminization of Poverty Series Video, 1987).

Teenage pregnancy and teenage parenting are huge social problems in terms of welfare and a literate citizenry. Rosemary Brown, former cabinet member of British Columbia, narrates the video *No Way! Not Me,* which provides a vital warning: unless young women take control of their lives and their careers, they face a bleak future of poverty and loneliness (Video, 1987).

It is important to realize that the amount and quality of a teenage mother's education is the single most important factor in determining the standard of living for her and her family. Rosemary Brown reminds teenagers that today's children need parents who are well educated. She implores them to get the best possible education, which will enable them to think, analyze, and make good choices (Video, 1987).

She challenges youth, saying, "This cycle of poverty must be broken. The feminization of poverty is a tragedy. It is a crisis that must be dealt with firmly and openly now" (Video, 1987).

"You are the generation who opened your wallets and your hearts to the starving children of the world. You are the generation who marches for peace and speaks out for justice. You see and understand the beauty and fragility of the planet, and care enough to try to protect it. You are better informed. You have more resources. You have more ability. You are more tolerant of peoples' differences; and you actually have better foundations on which to build than we ever did. I have confidence that you will take control of your lives, as you carefully, lovingly, yet firmly turn this world around until it reflects your highest aspirations and your dreams" (Video, 1987).

Objective: To discover the realities of poverty brought on by teenage pregnancy, divorce, and single parent family

PROJECT SHEET

HUMAN SEXUALITY AND THE PROSPECT OF POVERTY

RESEARCH PROJECTS. Individuals/small groups present a project: written/oral, skit, TV news, documentary.

1. RESEARCH THE TERM *POVERTY LINE*.
   a. What does it mean?
   b. How many families live below the poverty line?
   c. What are the causes for these conditions?
   d. How does it relate to teenage pregnancy? to divorce?

2. RESEARCH WOMEN'S SHELTERS. Interview someone at a women's shelter, a home for teenage mothers or social agency about:
   a. Pregnancy health care.
   b. How can a pregnant teenager get answers?
   c. What happens to teenage girls when they become a single parent?
   d. What happens to women and their families when their marriage breaks down?

3. RESEARCH PAY AND JOB OPPORTUNITIES: Woman/man who is a
   a. High school drop out
   b. High school graduate
   c. Semi-skilled worker
   d. Skilled worker
   e. Community college graduate
   f. Business college/technical school graduate
   g. Student who has had two years of college work
   h. College graduate
   i. Student who has done graduate studies and beyond

4. RESEARCH HELP AVAILABLE TO SOLVE PROBLEMS: In your life or one of your friends' lives. Where to find help. How to ask for what you want. What is free?

CHECK THE PUBLIC LIBRARY FOR INFORMATION ABOUT:
   a. Abuse
   b. Alcoholism/addiction
   c. Mental health and suicide
   d. Pregnancy health care
   e. Family crises
   f. Health care
   g. Legal matters

PLAN AHEAD FOR YOUR LIFE

A bright young woman,
A class leader,
returned to school her senior year pregnant.

In one of the seminars, one of those present was a student who embodied the strength and conviction needed by youth today. This young woman had a plan for her life. She had long-term goals. She also had the moral integrity to face her problems and make her life one of her own choosing. She showed that she could make decisions, accept what she could not change, and forge the future that she had planned. She was a bright young woman, a class leader, who returned to school her senior year, pregnant. To quiet the rumors, she asked to speak to her fellow students in the seminar. The title of her sharing was:

How It Is To Be As I Am At My Age

There was hush as she said, "I gave in to a moment of passion, and am now carrying the consequences of my actions.

"When I realized my condition, I felt trapped in a maze of conflicting decisions. For many weeks I told no one. I wasn't seeing the young man. It was summer. I had had time to plan.

"The dread I felt in the thought of telling my parents was overwhelming. I thought about abortion, but I knew that I could not kill my child. I considered suicide, but that, too, would take the baby's life.

"The only decision that I could live with was to face the pregnancy, bear the child, and place the child for adoption. I have many plans for my life, starting with a college degree.

"When I told my family, I saw so many emotions reflected upon their faces as the reality of my words were understood. My younger sisters turned pale. My grandmother was nonaccepting, asking, 'How could you?' It was the question that I had been asking myself for many weeks.

"I was so worried about returning to high school. I was afraid that the administration would not accept a returning student who was pregnant, so I applied to the university, but I was two credits short of their entrance requirements."

She smiled as she told of her feelings of relief when the principal welcomed her return.

"My confinement seems endless," she said. "Everything is different. The joys of youth are gone and have been replaced by worries and responsibilities.

"What about the baby? My mother has offered to raise the child as her own, so I can get on with my life, but this does not seem fair. My mother has raised a large family. This pregnancy is my problem and my responsibility. The only decision that I can live with is to face the pregnancy, bear my child, and place the infant for adoption.

"I thank you for accepting me as I am. I thank my friends who have remained constant and will listen as I pour out my heart. I ask you to pray with me that a deserving couple can be found to adopt my baby as their own, and give him or her the love, attention, and opportunities which are not mine now to give."

On Valentine's Day she gave birth to a baby boy. She stayed with her decision, and her baby was adopted.

Objective: To consider planning ahead for my life PROJECT SHEET

PLAN AHEAD FOR YOUR LIFE

A. What do you want to achieve with your life in terms of the following goals?

EDUCATION _____

OCCUPATION/CAREER _____

MARRIAGE _____

CHILDREN _____

LEISURE _____

RETIREMENT _____

OTHER _____

B. By 30 years old: which of the goals will you have achieved?

C. By 40 years old: which of the goals will you have achieved?

D. What must you do at this point in your life to ensure that your goals can be achieved?

E. How would your life plan change if you became: pregnant? a teenage parent? alcohol or drug dependent?

WRITE A SHORT ESSAY on one of the questions. Relate it to your life.

TOPIC: _____ DATE: _____

10 A WHY TO LIVE

OBJECTIVES:

1. To acknowledge suicide as a teenage problem
2. To consider reasons one might contemplate suicide
3. To discuss feelings and insights related to suicide
4. To consider ways to help a distraught person
5. To recognize the warning signs of suicide
6. To discuss ways suicide can be prevented
7. To consider a why to live

SUICIDE

A very serious young man used these words to describe someone who might contemplate suicide:

> "Alone, lost in the labyrinth
>   of pitfalls and traps
> set by an uncaring society..."

And in a poetic essay he wrote:

> "When one can see not a glimmer of hope,
> hear not the kind word of a loved one,
> feel not the warmth of another human being,
> then the wide door of suicide lies gaping open,
> ready to swallow the soul..."

Suicide is a huge teenage problem. Let us consider some facts about suicide from the Disease Control Center in Atlanta, Georgia:
- 5000 teens kill themselves annually
- 500,000 teens attempt suicide annually
- Suicide is the third most common form of teen death
- Three/fourths of would-be suicides indicate their intentions in some way
- A suicidal person is ambivalent, meaning the person has mixed feelings about living

High risk elements associated with teenage depression and suicide have been identified in recent studies. Feelings of great loss from the death of a parent or the loss of love from a parent through divorce are said to be the leading high risk elements in teenage depression and suicide. Children often experience feelings of abandonment and/or feelings of guilt that they might have been the cause of the parents' divorce.

Studies show that children who feel unloved or unwanted can feel expendable. However, there is never just one source of pressure. It is often the accumulation of stress from parents, friends, peer pressure, and school that can bring about the feeling of not being able to cope, and the desire for a way out of their problems.

Francine Klagsburn, in her book *Too Young To Die,* states that parents need information on suicide that emphasizes the importance of the early years in a child's development. She states that parents should be aware of the subtle ways a child can be made to feel unloved and unwanted. Not the least of these is not making time to listen to their questions and to show an interest in their friends and activities at school.

Rabbi Daniel Roberts of the Temple Emanuel in Cleveland states, in *Teenage Suicide,* that parents often view their children as status symbols rather than as human beings. They often neglect to express love, listen to their children's problems, or support them in trying times (Sandra Gardner and Gary Rosenberg).

David Richo, in *How To Be An Adult,* augments these thoughts, stating: "In a very real way, we are who we are because of the love others have shown us. Our every asset began as a gift from someone who loved us as we were, and thereby encouraged our unique self-emergence."

Childhood is short, and often teenage years are fragile. Pregnant teens may have to juggle misunderstandings at home as well as at school. Dr. Sol Gordon of the University of Syracuse, an expert on teenage sexuality, states, in the Gardner and Rosenberg book, that present day culture pushes teens into sexual relationships that they are not ready to handle emotionally. He states further that fear of or actual pregnancy is the largest single factor in teenage girls' attempts at suicide.

In *Crisis Counseling,* Eugene C. Kennedy reports that at least one half of all suicides are people suffering from depression when they take their lives.

Dorothy B. Francis, in *Suicide, A Preventable Tragedy,* tells us that scientists have found that sometimes depression has a physical foundation, a defect in the brain. Certain immune cells called lymphocytes may mimic brain cell defects in patients with depression. Clinical depression responds readily to treatment, but the medicine must be taken as prescribed. Today, a blood test is used to determine if a patient has lymphocytes.

Unless we have known someone who was depressed to the point of finding no other way to solve his or her problem(s) than to self-destruct, we might be judgmental. A person who has a good self-image and the positive support of both family and friends might find it difficult to understand a person's taking his or her own life.

Who is prone to become suicidal is still a big question. "The taking of one's life is an intensely personal act that occurs in all strata of society," writes Dorothy B. Francis. "There is no one typical suicidal youth." The ability to prevent this tragedy is as important as the reasons behind it.

STUDENT/DISCUSSION/ESSAY

Have you ever known anyone who threatened to commit, or actually committed suicide?

"A boy I worked with for three months committed suicide on Thursday morning. Nobody knows why." This statement of fact by a very upset girl brought the seminar class to order. "I wrote my feelings out in my journal," she said, "and I would like to share them with you.

"I went to the calling hours [at the funeral home], and in the short twenty minutes that I was there, I saw at least seventy kids from his school come and go. So many people were affected by the loss of his life, but he thought that he didn't matter.

"We mold ourselves out of little parts of all the people we love. So each person is made up of parts of others. People influence us by their personalities and their beliefs. When that person dies, a part of us is taken too.

"The boy who killed himself took with him so many aspects of people whom he probably never knew really cared."

When Lisa finished reading from her journal there was a hush. Jason responded, "Lisa, you make it sound as if you were somehow responsible for his death."

"Yes, Jason. That's the way I feel."

"But you said that the victim was just a working acquaintance on a part-time job where you work."

"Right, again, but that's how I feel. Suicide is such a waste of potential. Someone should have noticed...."

Greg spoke next: "I think that a person who wants attention, or who wants to scare his or her parents might consider suicide. I know someone who, eventually, admitted that she tried to kill herself for attention. No one had time for her. She felt unwanted and unloved."

Tom added, "I knew someone, too, who talked about suicide, because of the way his parents treated him. Nothing ever seemed to go his way. He was always in trouble. His parents even told him that he was a waste. He killed himself."

"Depressed, troubled, scared, confused, angry—these words describe a person who might be suicidal, like my friend. He's a neighbor, whose parents were going through a divorce," recalled Tim. "Frank, not his name, had been really depressed because his parents were constantly fighting when they were at home. During this time, Frank talked about killing himself. I told him that I would always be there for him, if he had a problem or needed to talk. Well, Frank's father earned all of the family money, so when he moved out, both Frank and his mom had to get jobs to support themselves. Frank got a job after school, and then Frank got a girlfriend. I know that he rarely thought of his parents when he was with her. She made a real difference."

It was Marcy's turn. "The words that come to my mind are similar to Greg's and Tom's. An insecure person who doesn't believe that anyone loves her might consider suicide. I thought of a friend. She was having problems at home with her parents. They were at odds over the boy she was dating, her time on the phone, and curfew. Then her grades fell and a deficiency note was sent home. To make matters worse, her boyfriend cut out. I was really worried about her. I was there for her. I listened."

"The words that come to my mind, to describe a person who might contemplate taking his life, are sell-out and quitter. I haven't known anyone who wanted to kill himself, but when life isn't going the way you want it to, it is easy to give up, to push things off, and not deal with reality. There are many outlets to channel your emotions rather than deal with them," said a self-confident young man. "I find nothing wrong with stopping the game of life for a few hours to have a couple of beers to release some stress, maybe catch a buzz. But when you commit suicide, you have finished the game of life. You have quit, given up. You are beat. I am not a quitter, and I will finish the game."

Melanie responded to Eric saying, "You sound like my dad. He's a very strong individual. He couldn't understand why my aunt would take her life. His sister was a loner. She had many problems and probably thought that no one could help."

Rob picked up the discussion, saying, "I know of a girl who committed suicide. She was the girlfriend of a friend of mine. He had gotten her pregnant freshman year. She had the baby sophomore year. She killed herself the beginning of her junior year. I'm not sure why she did it. Perhaps it was because she went from being very popular to being a social outcast. Towards the end they said that she spent a lot of time by herself."

Beth found the courage to speak up. "My twenty-year-old cousin committed suicide last year at the end of August. She was depressed and wouldn't take her medicine, because she thought that she was fine. Her father got into an argument with her about taking her medicine, and she ran away. She was missing for three days. We found her in the shed behind the garage. She had turned on the engine of her father's antique car, and died from carbon monoxide fumes. It was hard on all of us. Her parents were devastated. I still think about her. She will always be in my mind and heart."

Objectives: *To acknowledge suicide as a teenage problem*
              To consider reasons one might contemplate suicide
              To discuss feelings and insights related to suicide

EXERCISE/JOURNAL SHEET

SUICIDE

Comment on the following:

1. What reasons might a person have to contemplate suicide?

2. What words come to mind to describe a person who might contemplate suicide?

3. Have you ever known anyone who threatened to or actually did take his or her life?

WRITE A SHORT ESSAY: Use your descriptive words in #2 to begin your essay or CHOOSE A QUOTE from the readings. Cite an example. Relate it to someone you know.

TOPIC: _____ DATE: _____

Quote from Reading (pp._____) _____

HOW CAN SUICIDE BE PREVENTED?

A young teen handed in a poem, unsigned, which spoke of anguish:

> "My feelings get so distorted,
> > I don't know how to act sometimes.
>
> It makes me think I'm out of control
> > of my life.
>
> The times when I'm happy
> > everything looks beautiful, innocent;
>
> There is no evil in the world or
> > I don't see it.
>
> Maybe I don't want to.
> > Maybe my eyes are closed
> > and it's all a dream.
>
> The feelings of sadness,
> > depression, monotony
> > are born of the same father
>
> —one who knows only sorrow and
> > pain, pain."

When we write out our emotions, we are forced to read them—face up to our feelings. Perhaps this helped her. Listening to our peers we realize that each of us in our own way has a burden to carry. The courage of one often inspires another.

Stress plays a big part in the lives of all teenagers. So many decisions are pressed upon them in terms of what to do with their lives. Pressures from peers, parents, friends, job, and school surface in an ever increasing array. Some teens have special reasons for stress—some for reasons they did not try to control, some for reasons they could not control. Sometimes looking for a way out of problems causes mixed feelings about living.

The following helpful information is taken from a 1981 book published by the National Institute of Mental Health, Rockville, Maryland:

"Adolescence is the time between childhood and the young adult when teens question who we are and what life is. It is a time of turbulence with many changes taking place within us: physically, psychologically, emotionally, and socially. It is a time that is bound by many pressures: the family's desire for excellence that will lead to a good job and a well-established life; peer pressure to examine life now.

"The most beneficial pattern for mental health appears to be a balance between involvement with peers and remaining close with parents.

"Family disruption plays an important part in adolescent depression and suicidal behavior. Marital instability, economic stress, disruption of residence, and chronic, bitter conflict with parents can result in the feeling of being unloved and rejected. Poor grades, truancy, and disciplinary problems at school can be related factors.

"Suicidal individuals experience an increase in the number of life crises, stress and illness, coupled with a decrease in support from family and an inability to cope. However, we must keep in mind that the mere presence of crises and stress does not necessarily imply suicidal behavior."

There are warning signs of suicide of which we should be aware:
- lack of energy
- down-in-the-dumps demeanor
- loss of appetite or overeating
- neglect of personal appearance
- boredom
- withdrawal and isolation
- outbursts of anger
- obsession with death
- giving away special possessions
    —(Earl A. Grollman, *Suicide: Prevention, Intervention, Postvention*)

"A person who is in despair and tempted to take his own life needs a compassionate human being to whom he can say, 'Will you help me? Now?'" (Ibid).

John Langone, in his book *Dead End,* suggests the following as ways of preventing suicide:
- Be yourself with the distraught person.
- Listen. Listen for feelings.
- Talk...as an equal.
- Allow...unburdening without interruption.
- Ask simple, direct questions. No third degree.
- When you don't know what to say, say nothing.

Langone's suggested use of questions is to get the person to find personal answers. He admits that many times there is no answer, but the act of listening in itself bears witness to concern (Ibid).

If a cry is heard, a life might be saved. Listen and be aware of mood changes in your friends. It is not normal for teenagers to be constantly depressed, or to have mood swings for weeks. This may well be a cry for help. A loss of interest in their friends and regular activities, in their grades, and in their appearance are other indications of severe depression. The giving away of possessions, and finally the preoccupation with death and talk of suicide are the sure signals for help (Gardner/Rosenberg, *Teenage Suicide*).

So many social and psychological forces affect youth suicides that no single action can possibly solve the problem. Francine Klagsburn, in *Too Young to Die,* points to "the spiraling divorce rate, chaotic homes, confusion about religious beliefs and moral values, shrinking family groups, feelings of alienation between men and women, young and old that bring pressure, confusion and despair to young people."

Teenagers are sensitive and caring. They can appreciate the feelings of stress and disappointment, the possibility of guilt and shame, and the gauntlet of troubles stemming from peer pressure. They are aware of the insecurity when they think about who would understand, who would forgive. The listening and caring attitude of a friend can make a real difference when someone is upset.

There are always alternative choices, if we can get the distressed person to talk out his or her problems and consider a different approach to the crisis. If the depression persists, encourage the person to get professional help from a school counselor, a doctor, or clergyman—or call the *crisis hotline for suicide : 1-800-333-444*. The emergency number 911, is also available to help. It is important to relay information to a responsible person. *Suicide can be prevented.*

STUDENT DISCUSSION/ESSAY

Lisa opened the discussion. "My concern for my co-worker's taking his life is something that I won't soon forget. I have done a lot of thinking about it. We all need to accept ourselves, and we should help others to do the same. I think that it is very important to let people know about the goodness in them, to let them see their importance, and to make them feel that they are needed and accepted."

Ashley entered the discussion. "Lisa, maybe the guy needed to know that he was loved as well as needed. People need a reason to live."

Patrick disagreed. "I don't think you can make a person feel needed. If I'm not needed, I don't want someone trying to make me feel that I am. And I will find my own reason to live."

Erin gave her opinion: "I think that a person should be able to see their own goodness and importance, but I'm not sure how that happens."

"We only see ourselves as we think others see us." Sean offered.

"Then my show of appreciation of a person and sincere compliments would have a meaning?" Joan asked.

"Well, I think you need to pinpoint specific things about the person that are good and important," Sean answered.

Josh spoke up: "I feel that if someone really wants to kill himself, that person will talk about it to someone. That someone has the responsibility to get that person help before it's too late."

In a serious tone, a young man volunteered his ideas: "We must make ourselves available for people; listen to what they have to say; hear what they tell us, spoken and unspoken. In discussing suicide with my dad, who is a physician, he suggested that we should try to keep the distraught person talking. Ask them questions, like: Why are you unhappy? Who or what has made you upset? Is there someone I can get for you? Or: What can I do for you? Often, they will respond. Just from talking to someone who cares, the person may find ways to relieve their tensions, and find hope to go on. Dad also said that we should not leave them alone. Have someone get help, while we are talking to them. It would be good to check on the person, as a friend, after the incident."

Objectives: *To recognize that there are alternate solutions to one's problems* EXERCISE/JOURNAL SHEET
To recognize the warning signs of suicide
To discuss ways suicide can be prevented

HOW CAN SUICIDE BE PREVENTED?

1. Give alternate solutions to the problems you cited as reasons to contemplate taking one's life.

2. How can suicide be prevented?

3. What are the warning signs of suicide?

4. What should be done when the warning signs of suicide are recognized in a distraught person?

WRITE A SHORT ESSAY on one of the topics or CHOOSE A QUOTE from the readings. Relate it someone you know.

TOPIC: _____ DATE: _____

Quote from Reading (pp._____) _____

A WHY TO LIVE

Students are challenged to think about life
and their reasons for living.

STUDENTS DISCUSSION/ESSAY

That which does not kill me makes me stronger.
—Nietzsche

A happy, vivacious girl opted to open the sharings. "As many of you know, cheerleading has been a major part of my life. When we had try-outs for this year, I felt pretty sure that I would make it again. But I didn't. I don't ever remember feeling so low in all my life. I was literally crushed. I even thought about killing myself because I felt that I had nothing to live for. The worst part was that I had school the next morning. I debated about going, but I knew I had to go. The experience showed me who my friends were and how much they cared. It also showed me that I can take it not to succeed all the time." She seemed relieved to confess this.

A quiet student followed. "I have grown extremely strong in myself and by my own will because of past experiences. I won't go into detail, but as a child, I experienced serious mental pain because of the actions of my brothers, sisters and parents. I have found that by experiencing so much anguish early in life, it has built my character, will and strength to handle problems. I feel that something positive can always result. One can always learn from mistakes, and when I'm faced with a problem, I feel something positive can always result."

Then an earnest young man gave two short but pointed examples of the meaning of the Nietzsche quotation for his life. He said, "If you break up with your girlfriend, you will hurt, but you will gain experience from it." And: "I feel like I'm going to die at wrestling practice because it is so hard, but it makes me a stronger person." His last remark brought laughter.

Aaron was next to speak. "Maybe this quotation fits some people's situation but not mine. The last few days, I've seen my father go through the pain of watching his brother have a stroke and lose most of his mental capabilities. I have seen him gain hope at his brother's fast recovery, only to learn yesterday of another stroke, causing a blood clot to his brain. As I took my father to the airport this morning, I could see that this was not making him any stronger at all. It will not kill him to watch his only brother die, but it definitely will not make him any stronger either."

"Aaron, I'm sorry about your uncle and your dad," Cindy put in. "But in your own pain from watching your father, you are thinking about his physical strength. Emotionally, your dad will be stronger. You must be very proud of him."

"Yeah. I am."

He who has a why to live can bear almost any how.
—Nietzsche

Carol smiled as she spoke: "The best why in my life is another person. If you have someone to love and that someone loves you, this is reason enough to give meaning to life."

A somber youth was next to speak: "In the past five years, I have had to struggle to get through life because of a broken family. Whenever I felt down I would look ahead and think of all the good things to come. I will live my way around any hardship to realize my dream."

A young man was reminded of an older woman, Rosie, who had had cerebral palsy since birth. "She has lived her life in a wheelchair. She goes to my church and is very devout. She has been able to get through life by her faith in God. She has been able to live with the how because of her why to live. This is the example that I have seen through my life."

Mike had given much thought to his essay relating to his why to live, and offered to read it. "In a Christian sense this quote dictates my personal belief about each person's relationship to God. Everyone has a purpose. Each person has a duty to live his life to serve a purpose whether it be for a multi-billion-dollar firm or as a skid row bum. Each person touches another, offering some happiness. I think of a solitary old man feeding pigeons in the park. If he ceases to do this feeding, those with whom he came into contact will experience a loss—maybe it will be a child.

"This concept of having a role to fill, even if we dislike our role, should compel us to continue striving for life—to finish our purpose. Oftentimes when I'm depressed, I fail to see a purpose, but I keep striving.... When I was choosing a college and a career, I decided to take things as they came, confident that God would ultimately lead me. I don't know what my why is, but I know there is one—an important one for me alone to conquer."

Is life fair?

A charismatic young man often drew the group together. Steve changed from his sitting position into a coach's stance, crouching. He looked around the circle of friends and read his essay:

"Life is as fair as a foul ball on chalk. Life is as fair as getting one foot inbounds; blocking a shot and getting a foul; eating the frosting off the cake and getting caught. In all of the above situations, there is a good and a bad. You can make life fair by looking at a glass one-half full and not one-half empty. You must remember happy times and that there always is a way."

Objective: To consider a why to live EXERCISE/JOURNAL SHEET

A WHY TO LIVE

For a person with a happy heart and a secure home it is hard to imagine a person committing suicide. Yet it happens every day. It happens to young people. The increasing number of youth suicides nationwide challenges us to think about LIFE.

Comment on the following:

1. That which does not kill me makes me stronger. —Nietzsche

2. He who has a why to live can bear almost any how. —Nietzsche

3. Is life fair?

WRITE A SHORT ESSAY on one of the quotations or CHOOSE A QUOTE from the readings. Relate it to yourself or to someone you know. Cite an example.

TOPIC: _____ DATE: _____

Quote from Reading (pp._____) _____

11 A WORD CAN MEAN SO MUCH

OBJECTIVES:

1. To recognize the importance of courteous behavior
2. To experience the power of *please* and *thank you*
3. To share the experience of saying, "I love you"
4. To appreciate the importance of showing affection
5. To share the experience of saying, "I'm sorry"

As soon as children begin to talk, parents are eager to teach them to say *please* and *thank you* at the proper times. In fact, these expressions rank with *I love you* and *I'm sorry* as a learned art in communication.

Acquiring an attitude of courteous behavior is a lesson of great importance in developing good human relations. Without *please*, a favor becomes a demand or a command, and all sense of social behavior goes awry. People who start sentences with verbs such as: *do, go, get, bring,* give the impression of asking servitude from others. Age has no privilege. Parents who want to be obeyed should employ the kindness in their words that invites an eagerness to comply.

THE POWER OF *PLEASE* AND *THANK YOU*

Does the way in which someone speaks to us affect the way we feel about them? People who are popular and well-liked have learned how to get along with others. They treat others with respect. They are courteous. The few words that help to make this possible are *please* and *thank you*. We open the discussion by recalling an experience when someone's saying *please* made a difference, or when someone's saying *thank you* was the best possible payment we could imagine.

STUDENT DISCUSSION/ESSAY

Stephen, a sixteen-year-old junior from a family of five, spoke first. "This weekend I washed the family car without being asked. When I told my dad, he shouted, 'It's about time! You use it often enough.' If he had just said, 'Thanks,' I would have been happy, because I knew that he was pleased. It will be a while before I wash the car for him again."

"He sounds like my dad, Steve," said Jill. "One night at dinner, my brother reached across the table for the potatoes, and got his hand slapped. 'Say please pass the potatoes,' my father said, loudly. 'This is not a boarding house!' Sometimes our fathers hurt us just as we sometimes hurt others. Other times, it's just their way of teaching us good manners."

"Hey, that explains the expression 'the boarding house reach'!" put in Tom. Laughter followed his comment.

"My mom said that she can still remember the first time I said *thank you* without being reminded. She told me that it seemed as important to her as taking my first step!" laughed Kim.

Anxious to share her observations Kelly waved her hand to be recognized. "I tried the survey questions on my little niece. Even a two-year-old resents being commanded to do something. I also found that the tone of voice I used made a big difference. When I asked Megan in a persuasive tone, 'Bring Auntie Kelly her sweater from the chair,' she was hesitant. When I added 'Please?' she broke into a smile and toddled to the chair to get it."

"I had worked very hard with the stage crew for the musical. I was asked to do murals on the backdrops and they really came out well. But because the student vocalists are in the spotlight of such events, I felt that my contribution was overlooked. A simple 'thank you' would have helped the night of the show. Since that experience, I make it a point to express my thanks even for little things," recalled a senior man.

"The manager where I work never fails to tell us 'good job' or something positive. It makes such a difference in the way I feel about myself and my job," asserted Ed.

"I feel like a different person when I'm at my friend's house. They say *please* and *thank you* with the same ease that my kid brother says, 'Give me that. It's mine.' He has other expressions that I'd rather not mention. He embarrasses me and he doesn't care," admitted a junior girl. "My dad says that he's just going through a stage. I hate it."

"At our house, we often talk about courtesy on the roadways. I just got my license and my sister hasn't had hers that long. We always notice if the person whom we have allowed to pull out in front of us, or such, waves or gives us a high sign as thanks. Some do and others don't. But I always feel so pleased if a person acknowledges my kindness," Heather added.

Objectives: *To recognize the importance of courtesy in dealing with people* EXERCISE/JOURNAL SHEET
To appreciate the importance of gratitude

THE POWER OF *PLEASE* and *THANK YOU*

1. Report on a survey where you a) ask a favor, b) tell someone to do something, and c) command an action. Note who it was, what was said, his or her reactions and yours.

   Your request statement: _____ (Example: "Hand me the newspaper.")

2. How does the way someone speaks to you affect the way you feel about that person?

3. Recall an experience when *please* made a difference, or *thank you* was the best possible payment for a favor given.

4. In which identity do you often experience gratitude? What effect does appreciation have on you?

5. Saying *please* and *thank you* is more than courtesy; it is a reflection of our person. Do you agree with this statement? Why/Why not?

WRITE A SHORT ESSAY on one of the topics, or CHOOSE A QUOTE from the readings. Relate it to self/another. Cite an example. Include their reactions and yours.

TOPIC: _____ DATE: _____

Quote from Reading (pp._____) _____

THREE LITTLE WORDS: I LOVE YOU

Love is a very fragile thing
- a word can put the heart on wing,
- be the sun on a dreary day,
- lighten our step or show the way,
- or take from life all gloss and glow
- the sharpest pain life can bestow.

So often we vent our anger and frustration, and find it hard to reaffirm our love. It is very important that we learn to express our feelings of affection. Sharing words of endearment can mean so much.

Greeting cards or, better yet, personal notes that carry the message of gratitude or of love are very important to us. They are often read and reread, because they fill us with the joy of being appreciated, or of being loved.

However, hearing endearing words holds an even greater meaning. Voice inflection can be etched in our memory, and our mind can capture every nuance. To hear something nice said to us is to let us see it in our mind's eye, and hold the meaning in our hearts. Those of us who come from caring, demonstrative families are accustomed to saying "I love you" to each other. We can't fake caring, but we can learn to be caring, and our expressions of love will enrich our lives and the lives of those we touch.

In any language, words hold great power in the life of every person. To the question, "Which words hold the greatest power?" students were quick to respond.

STUDENT DISCUSSION/ESSAY

A bright youth with a wide grin spoke up to answer: "Well, depending upon when they are said, how they are said, and to whom they are said, the words would have to be 'I love you.'"

"I think the words would be 'I'm sorry!'" challenged Cindy. "If you have ever been really hurt, emotionally that is, 'I'm sorry' can mean as much or more than 'I love you.'"

Mary, an outgoing, vivacious teen, who shared joy with those around her, waved to speak. "My dad died suddenly, earlier this year. There was no chance to say goodbye. But the memory of sharing the words 'I love you' with him each night since childhood has helped me."

Carla, a serious student and an outstanding athlete, spoke quietly: "My dad died this year, too. Last year we knew that he was dying of cancer, yet he came to all of our varsity girls' basketball games. He seemed to gain strength in our success. He even saw our team win the state title." As she recounted her feelings of loss, she added, "He knew that I loved him, and I knew that he loved me. We just never said it in words. Now I wish that I had. I think that it would have eased my loss. One thing I did do that helped was to go back to church."

Daniel, who was shy and unsure of himself, admitted, "It was a great relief to me to say 'I love you' to each of my parents. I had wanted to tell them. They were surprised—and pleased. Afterwards, I felt that a heavy weight had been lifted."

"My experience was different," said another young man. "I visited my grandmother who is battling cancer. She seemed to enjoy my company, and was happy that I spent some time with her. She told me that she loved me and was proud of me. I wish that I had told her I loved her, too."

"I said 'I love you' to my three-year-old nephew, Billy, because I knew he would accept it. He gave me a big hug and a kiss," Richard confessed.

One young man added a light touch. "When I told my mother 'I love you,' she thought I wanted money, and told me to do my homework! I should have told her that it was an assignment." His remarks brought laughter.

"I don't say 'I love you' to just anyone," Brian stated resolutely. "I'm saving the words to be said to someone very special for a life commitment."

"Brian, words of affection are not like currency to be saved or spent!" a feisty blonde charged. "In the lives of most people, 'I love you' needs to be heard, needs to be taken in, and emotionally savored. Day-to-day living can be so hard to bear. I know, because I have seen it in my mother, since my dad left."

Then Dawn had the courage to speak. "My mom was feeling down one morning when I left for school. On my first free period, I phoned her and said, 'I love you, Mom.' She thanked me and added that she loved me, too. When I got home, she gave me a hug and thanked me again."

From across the circle, a male voice added: "The other day, before I left for school, my mom said, 'I love you.' So I said 'I love you' back as I was walking out. Then I went back into the kitchen, and she looked at me with a surprised expression on her face!"

A very gentle girl spoke next. "Saying 'I love you' is difficult for me. For some reason, when I was younger showing emotions was considered babyish. So now I really have to work at it. My parents don't say it. But my sister and I are best friends. We talk about everything, so when I told her that I loved her, she told me back. We hugged."

Objective: To discuss the experience of saying "I love you"   EXERCISE/JOURNAL SHEET

THREE LITTLE WORDS: I LOVE YOU

In this exercise you are to experience your feelings as you affirm your love for someone, and recall your feelings when someone expressed his or her love for you.

1. Have you ever told someone "I love you"?

    How did it make you feel?

2. Has anyone ever said to you, "I love you"?

    How did it make you feel?

3. Tell someone whom you love: "I love you."

WRITE A SHORT ESSAY on one of the topics, or CHOOSE A QUOTE from the readings. Relate it to your life or to someone you know. Cite an example. Include your reactions and theirs.

TOPIC: _____ DATE: _____

Quote from Reading (pp._____) _____

TWO BIG WORDS: I'M SORRY

> Decide to forgive
> > for resentment is negative
> > resentment is poisonous
> > resentment diminishes and devours self.
>
> Be the first to forgive, to smile and to
> > take the first step
>
> And you will see happiness bloom on the face
> > of your human brother or sister.
>
> Be always the first
> > do not wait for others to forgive
> > for by forgiving you become
> > the master of fate,
> > the fashioner of life
> > the doer of miracles.
>
> To forgive is the highest, most beautiful
> > form of love....
> > > —Robert Muller, former assistant secretary-general of the
> > > United Nations (Christopher News Notes, 1992)

Saying the words "I'm sorry" is to ask forgiveness. Though it is an admission of wrong doing, it is also an expression of regret. A sincere apology often removes the feelings of resentment, and provides a means of salvaging a relationship.

We have all been hurt or have known misunderstandings in our families, between friends or with employees on the job. We are aware, then, of the need at times to mend our personal relationships. A sincere apology is one of the surest ways to make amends.

An apology can remove the feelings of guilt that accompany a wrong or a misunderstanding. It can restore tranquillity and permit the injured party the opportunity to forgive. The act of forgiveness removes our feelings of resentment, and often deepens the awareness of our relationship.

There may be a risk in saying "I'm sorry," prompted by the fact that our apology may be rejected. If we grew up in a family where a parent was bitter and negative, we may have been spurned so often by callous, verbal treatment that we would naturally be cautious in inviting any comment on our actions.

As we plan our lives, there are cycles that we want to break, and there should also be patterns of action that we want to develop. Learning the art of communication should be one of them. We can show respect for others by being courteous. We can make a difference in the way we relate to others, by saying *please* and *thank you*. We can make a difference in the way we relate to those we love by saying *I love you* and *I'm sorry*.

STUDENT DISCUSSION/ESSAY

Carl opted to start the discussion. "It's not hard for me to say that I'm sorry. If I wrong someone, I feel guilty, and I feel the need to say it."

Sharon said, "I'd been at odds with my mom, and I hadn't spoken to her for a couple of days. Then after school, I found my favorite candy bar on my dresser. It made me smile. The candy bar made it possible for me to go to her. When I said I was sorry, she hugged me."

Doug, whose sharings always showed an openness and good humor, said, "I apologized to my dad for getting a speeding ticket. But it took more than just saying I was sorry to prove to him that I was serious."

"I took my brother's bike after school without asking him, and didn't get back until dinnertime. I didn't know that he had planned to use it. He was furious, until I said 'I'm sorry.' Maybe that's why I remember the incident."

Gerry was waving something that she held in her hand. "I brought in this comic strip from *Better or Worse*. It is so fitting for today's assignment. I'll pass it around," she said.

For Better or For Worse®   by Lynn Johnston

"I really liked your sharing, Gerry. It kind of fits in with what I am going to say," said a thoughtful young woman. "My friend at work and I had a fight. It was her fault, but after a few days of not speaking, I was miserable. I told her when I apologized that I like her better as a friend than as an enemy."

A shy girl said, "If my mom and dad have an argument, I get so nervous. But one good thing is that they never go to bed angry. It's usually my dad who apologizes."

"I stayed at Grandma's house during the day, before I started to school, because my mom worked. My grandma taught me to say *I'm sorry* and *Excuse me* interchangeably over little things. If I walked in front of someone to get out of a church pew, or along a row in a theater, or if I bumped into someone accidentally...."

Before she could finish, someone broke in with, "Yes, me too. I remember reaching across my friend to get a piece of candy and hearing, 'Robert Albert! what should you say?' I didn't know whether to respond 'Excuse me' or 'Please pass the candy!'" The teenager was laughing heartily over the memory.

In his essay, a young man who spoke often of his four brothers, recalled an incident when he asked forgiveness. "All I heard was a big splash as my water balloon exploded. I darted from the deck into the house, and walked slowly into the TV room, where some of my family were talking. Suddenly a younger brother burst into the room. He had been my moving target as he mowed my grandparents' lawn with the tractor."

'Whoever threw that is dead! The water balloon hit Granddad, and it got mud all over his shirt!'

"Where had granddad come from? I hadn't seen him! I was full of fear as I heard his approaching footsteps. Granddad stopped at the entrance of the room and roared, 'Who threw the water balloon?'

"'I did,' I admitted, 'but I wasn't aiming at you, honest.'

"Granddad took me aside. Before he could say anything, I blurted out, 'I'm sorry. I promise never to mess around with my brothers in your presence again!' He hugged me. Forgiveness feels so good."

Objective: To discuss the experience of saying, "I'm sorry"   EXERCISE/JOURNAL SHEET

TWO BIG WORDS: I'M SORRY

Saying "I'm sorry" is to ask for forgiveness. Though an admission of wrong doing, it is also an expression of regret. It may help to remove the feeling of resentment and provide a means of salvaging a relationship.

1. Apologize to someone to whom you owe an apology, or recall an incident when you apologized.

2. Recall when someone's apology held great meaning to you.

WRITE A SHORT ESSAY on one of the topics or CHOOSE A QUOTE from the readings. Cite an example. Relate it to yourself. Include the effect on you/other person.

TOPIC: _____ DATE: _____

Quote from Reading (pp._____) _____

12 GIVING AND RECEIVING

OBJECTIVES:

1. To realize that we can bring joy to others
2. To acknowledge the importance of gratitude
3. To recognize the value of receiving compliments well
4. To recognize that a sincere compliment is a gift
5. To recognize the importance of complimenting others

GIVING AND RECEIVING

Children, perhaps, give the finest example of receiving gifts well. Their joy abounds in the excitement of removing the wrappings. Their faces reflect the magic of surprise. Their voices shout their delight! Often they hold the toy or clothing tightly to themselves, and they share their excitement with others: "Look what Uncle Bill got for me!" The gratitude of children shown by words and tight embraces makes giving to children rewarding.

Childhood is short and too soon we lose this talent for uninhibited joy. In most of us this exuberance never returns. However, we can keep this joy in our lives if we choose to, for it is an attitude toward life that can be developed.

Viktor Frankl, in his book *Man's Search for Meaning*, tells of being profoundly moved by a kindness while a prisoner in a German concentration camp:

> ... it was far more than the small piece of bread which moved me to tears at the time. It was the human 'something' which this man gave to me—the word and look which accompanied the gift.

We are capable of showing joy and appreciation in many ways. People can read it in our eyes, detect it in our smile, feel it in our touch, hear it in our voice, and sense it in our manner of giving and receiving. In the beautiful prayer of St. Francis are the words "... for it is in giving that we receive..." which tell us that a gift well received can bring as much joy to the giver as the gift itself brings to the one receiving it. A gift poorly received, on the other hand, is a form of rejection. The hurt is measured by the love that made us care.

STUDENT DISCUSSION/ESSAY

Andrew was anxious to start the discussion. "When I was twelve years old, my family went to Myrtle Beach for vacation. I bought my grandmother a present there. It was a shell and inside hung a bell. It was lovely. Somehow with all of our stuff it got broken. I told my grandmother about it. She looked excited. Then I said, 'It got broken, but I'll buy you something else.' She smiled and gave me a big hug saying, 'You have given me a present. You thought of me on your trip, that is present enough.' She made me feel so good."

"I always buy my nieces' presents early, because it's fun. They get so excited and are so easy to please," recalled Debbie.

"My little cousin gave me this key ring for my birthday. The logo that hangs from it is my favorite team. But the reason that it means so much to me is because of his pride and joy when he gave it to me. He had wrapped it himself and made a special card. He told me I would like it." Andy smiled as he put his key ring back in his pocket.

In an essay a student told of her mother's buying a watch for her dad for Christmas. "Mom had planned the gift well in advance, because it meant saving a dollar a week from her grocery money. It was a splendid watch. A neighbor who was a jeweler had gotten it for her at a special price, and recommended it highly. Christmas morning Mom went to church after we kids opened our presents. She hurried back. When Mom came in, Dad told her that my aunt had called. Aunt Betty wanted to know how he liked his watch. That was the only reference he made to the gift. My mother was crushed. She said that she would never plan such a special gift for him again."

A hesitant young woman took her turn to speak. "I know how it feels when there is no appreciation, or joy shown when receiving a gift. I remember specifically a time when I gave a gift that was poorly received. Every Christmas my brother, sister, and I go over to my dad's house to open presents. That Christmas things had not been going well between me and my stepmother, and me and my dad. I was very uncomfortable about going over to their house. I was in the eighth grade. I wanted to get something good that I thought they would like. I bought a twenty dollar gift box of different kinds of chocolates at a fancy candy store.

"Well, they hated it! My dad said that he couldn't believe that I bought him candy. My stepmother said that it was a very inconsiderate thing to do. Two days later, I found out that my dad took the candy to his office and gave it to his secretaries. I was very hurt. This increased my dislike for my stepmother. I could not believe the things they said and did. I determined to stay away from both of them."

A boy spoke up and put things in perspective when he said, "Rejection by a parent hurts so badly because we still need to know that we are loved."

Objectives: *To recognize we are capable of bringing joy by the way we treat others*
To appreciate the impact of rejection
To appreciate the impact of gratitude

EXERCISE/JOURNAL SHEET

GIVING AND RECEIVING

1. Did you ever feel that you received more than you gave?

2. Recall a gift that was graciously received.

3. Recall a special gift that was poorly received.

4. Comment on "... for it is in giving that we receive...." —St. Francis of Assisi

WRITE A SHORT ESSAY on one of the topics or CHOOSE A QUOTE from the readings. Relate it to yourself/someone you know. Cite an example. Note your reactions and that of others.

TOPIC: _____ DATE: _____

Quote from Reading (pp._____) _____

_____
_____
_____
_____
_____
_____
_____
_____
_____
_____
_____
_____
_____
_____
_____
_____
_____
_____
_____
_____
_____
_____
_____
_____
_____
_____
_____
_____
_____
_____
_____
_____
_____
_____
_____
_____

WHAT DO YOU DO WITH A COMPLIMENT?

On a daily basis we make many choices in terms of receiving and rejecting gifts from others. Perhaps we don't think of a compliment in terms of a gift. A compliment is a verbal gift, a gift of praise. Often, in memory, we prize a sincere compliment longer that any material gift. We all need recognition—whether it is about how we look, what we have done, or what we have achieved. A compliment is life-giving.

As people in general, and as teenagers in particular, we develop a "look" for ourselves in terms of style, haircut, makeup, and clothes. Young women admit to spending a great deal of time to achieve their desired look before going to school. Some are eager to get a job as soon as they are sixteen, and in many cases the monies earned are spent on clothes, which they hope will make a "this is me" statement for them. Survey results on receiving compliments, then, in many cases are deceiving. Since young women in particular spend so much time attaining their "look," one might assume that they would be pleased to receive praise. This fact is only partly true.

A survey on receiving compliments shows that most teenagers find it difficult to accept compliments. They have a poor self-image. They don't believe that they are worthy of the praise, and they question the reason anyone would admire them.

John Powell, author of *Free To Be Me*, states: "When someone gives you a compliment, life is questioning you.... If you can't take a compliment, if you can't let someone get close to you, if you are terrified of intimacy, ask yourself what you really believe about yourself. ...If you do believe in yourself, you will have few problems with compliments...."

STUDENT DISCUSSION/ESSAY

A young woman read her comments: "What do I do with a compliment? I can accept them, though I feel shy afterwards. But I do like receiving them. A sincere compliment makes me feel very much alive and noticed. The way I react toward the person who gives me a compliment depends on who it is. Most of the compliments that I receive are about my looks. I give compliments, but only when they are honest."

A young man said: "I don't accept compliments very well. My reaction to a person who gives me a compliment is to feel humble. The compliments I receive are generally about my nice personality. I give compliments on occasion."

A smiling young woman signaled to share next. "I love to hear compliments from others. They make me feel out of this world. Most of my compliments are from my friends. I give compliments on a regular basis because I can make someone's day a lot better."

David said, "I have found giving compliments a positive experience. It gives me a good feeling about myself to give a good feeling to others."

"A sincere compliment makes me feel that I have done something right. I think complimenting people is positive. I not only make people feel good, but I feel good as well," said John confidently.

"When you say something nice to a person, the person is sometimes surprised, but you both feel good. I should do it more often. Only when someone cannot accept a compliment is it hard. It's hard because they don't feel good about it, and you feel rejected." Terry had obviously given some thought to his comments.

Objective: To recognize the value of receiving compliments well

EXERCISE/JOURNAL SHEET

WHAT DO YOU DO WITH A COMPLIMENT?

All people need recognition, whether it's for how they look, what they have done, or what they have achieved.

1. Do you accept a compliment well? Explain.

2. How does a sincere compliment make you feel?

3. Generally how do you act toward the person who gives you the compliment?

4. For which aspect of your personality do you receive the most compliments? Does this fact surprise you?

5. Do you give compliments on a regular basis? Why?/Why not?

6. Do you think you will be more willing to give more compliments in the future? Why?

WRITE A SHORT ESSAY on a topic above or recall a compliment that you received that meant a lot to you. Was it the person who said it? what was said? or both?

TOPIC: _____ DATE: _____

WHAT DO OTHER PEOPLE DO WITH COMPLIMENTS?

We often hear of the act of giving compliments expressed as *paying* compliments. In the dictionary the word *pay* is defined as giving (to a person) what is due. If we really believe in ourselves, then we can accept the compliments that are due us and grow from the love engendered by them.

How many people can and do really accept the praise given to them? Student survey results show that young people, for the most part, are embarrassed when complimented and put down the person who offered it, or in some way show a negative attitude toward receiving a compliment. If this is the way young people treat the friends who admire them, what kind of a relationship are they establishing?

Compliments to a casual acquaintance in many instances fare no better. Many people will not accept compliments. Their refusal to accept praise reflects their own poor self-image and immaturity. More than that, a flippant response to a sincere expression of approval is taken as a put down by the one who offered the praise. It is a rejection of that person.

It is cause for wonder why family members put each other down so often. In developing a positive attitude toward life, home is a great starting place. We should give compliments to family members on a regular basis. When we think of something nice to say to each other, we should say it. Words of praise can bring happiness and joy. Where better to start than at home?

Accepting compliments graciously comes with accepting ourselves, with being able to say thanks for the gift, with being able to say to ourselves, "Yes, that is true!"

Giving compliments is one of the many ways that we can reach out to others and touch them with that human "something"—a word or a look that reaches to the heart.

STUDENT DISCUSSION/ESSAY

Students investigate the responses to specific compliments given to friends, acquaintances and family members.

"You look nice" is the compliment most often given to a friend or family member, with the response generally being a smile and a thank you.

But some ungracious or embarrassed responses might include a nervous laugh, a sarcastic look, a look of disbelief, or statements such as: Oh, really? Liar! Yeah, right. You're joking. What brought *that* on?

"I told my mom the dinner was great. She immediately got up from the table, wrote the compliment on a Post-it Note and stuck it to the refrigerator door. 'I can live on this for a week!' she said."

"When I told Joe how good his speech was, he said 'Thank you, but I thought it stunk,'" Amy said with a shrug.

"I told a girl who sits next to me in math class that I liked her sweater. She gave me a strange look, then said, 'Thanks.' I won't bother to notice her again. I felt like I had egg on my face," confessed Adam.

"I know what you mean. I told an acquaintance that her hair looked nice, and she snapped, 'No, it doesn't.'"

"Yeah, it hurts when they put you down. I told my brother, 'Nice paint job.' He said nothing. It was like my words were left hanging in the air."

Matt smiled as he spoke: "You're telling so many downers! I found giving compliments was mainly positive. I like to hear good things about myself, and I found that most other people did, too."

"I told a friend, 'Nice job on that test.' Just the way he said 'Thanks,' I knew he felt proud and happy that I noticed," Sandy reported.

"My compliments have been well received, too. I feel that a compliment lets someone know that I admire and respect them in some way," explained Mike.

"I like to make people feel good about themselves," Michelle put in. "Giving compliments is a good way to do that."

"People like to hear good things about themselves. When they smile or compliment you back, it makes you feel good about yourself." Steve put it all together.

Objective: To recognize the importance of complimenting others   EXERCISE/JOURNAL SHEET

WHAT DO OTHER PEOPLE DO WITH COMPLIMENTS?

Recall three compliments you remember giving.

Record the compliment, the reaction, and your reaction when you complimented:

    A friend:

    A family member:

    A casual acquaintance:

Comment on each experience. Was it positive or negative? Explain.

Have you ever been complimentary about someone to others, yet never paid the compliment to that person? Why?

WRITE A SHORT ESSAY on one of the experiences above or CHOOSE A QUOTE from the readings. Include an example. Note your reaction and that of the other person.

TOPIC: _____ DATE: _____

Quote from Reading (pp. _____) _____

13 HAPPINESS FOR ME

OBJECTIVES:

1. To discover gifts of the moment that bring happiness
2. To consider what makes people happy
3. To recognize that I am responsible for my own happiness
4. To recognize that happiness is a choice

> A tiny bunch of dandelions
>   picked in early spring,
> Clutched by warm, fat fingers
>   what happiness they bring—
> Smiling butter 'neath the chin
>   of the cherub proud,
> Who races to his mother
>   to shout his love out loud!

HAPPINESS LOG AND SURVEY

How many of us are aware of the happy moments in the days of our lives? These need not be pleasures of great size or value, of outstanding worth, or incredible good fortune. Happiness often comes in prized moments of remembrance, in sharing another's joy, in earned recognition, in the coincidence of good fortune, in forgiving ourselves or being forgiven by another.

Happiness is known in peace of heart, in peace of mind, in peace in the family, and between friends. Happiness is a joy in the heart in the knowledge of a job well done, in selecting the perfect gift for a friend, in paying a sincere compliment, in being proud of our actions, in showing respect. Happiness can be a simple joy, a single kindness, an act of faith, a sign of hope, a moment of prayer. Happiness comes from the wise choices we make on a day-to-day basis.

To gain an awareness of the gifts of the moment, an exercise in keeping a daily log (for one week) may bring the realization that happiness can be attained in both giving and receiving. Asking family members and friends the meaning of happiness for them is an occasion to share and become aware of the sensitivities of others.

STUDENT DISCUSSION/ESSAY

Ryan opened the discussion:
Monday: I learned that my grandmother does not have a brain tumor.
Tuesday: I made $40.00 caddying.
Wednesday: My mom told me that she loved me.
Thursday: My sister received government aid.
Friday: I got an A on a test.
Saturday: I got a date for the Senior Prom.

Alison was next to share her log:
Monday: My friend was accepted for college.
Tuesday: I made up with one of my friends.
Wednesday: I took a friend for a hot fudge sundae.
Thursday: My dad got called back to work.
Friday: Received compliments on the skirt I made.
Saturday: Started my new job.

Jesse turned the discussion to his survey of what brought happiness to his family and friends:
My dad: Happiness is a family that can get along; a family that is full of love.
My friend, Ethan: Happiness is being content in knowing that there are friends that you can count on.
My friend, Mike: Happiness is a loving relationship.
My brother, 12: Playing baseball.
My sister, Megan, 4: Playing with Barbie dolls.

Bryan offered the results of his survey:
Mom is happy when she doesn't have any worries about the children or about finances.
Dad said that he had a happy day at work because there were few problems. He was also happy as he opened the door and smelled the pot roast, and liked having everyone together for dinner.
Pete is happy when he gets good grades on his tests.
Mikey, 11, is happy when he's eating spaghetti.
My friend, Rich, relates happiness to his family and friends, especially his friends. He likes to shoot hoops and get a burger with them—and likes just being together.
My friend, Jenni, said happiness is receiving a smile while passing someone in the hall, getting a compliment, sharing a laugh, being with a good friend.

Alli waved to be recognized: "I'll just read what people said when I asked what made them happy, if that's okay:
When the computer program works.
When the ironing is done.
Seeing my parents in a good mood after their work.
No homework on a sunny day.
Going out with friends and playing sports.
Being in a comfortable, secure place.
Visits from my dad.
Creating new drawings.

Objectives: To discover gifts of the moment that bring happiness for me
To consider what makes other people happy

EXERCISE/JOURNAL SHEET

HAPPINESS LOG

Enter moments of a day(or days) that were special to you. Try it for a week. Take note: were you giving/receiving?

Day/Date   *What Took Place?*   *Were You Giving/Receiving?*

HAPPINESS SURVEY

Survey questions:
  What does happiness mean to you?
  Who is responsible for your happiness?

ASK TWO ADULTS TO ANSWER THE QUESTIONS: (designate relationship)

  First Adult:

  Second Adult:

ASK TWO TEENAGERS TO ANSWER THE QUESTIONS:

  First Teen:

  Second Teen:

ASK A CHILD WHAT MAKES HIM OR HER HAPPY

  Answer:

WRITE A SHORT ESSAY on a topic above or CHOOSE A QUOTE from the readings. Cite an example. Relate to self/other.

TOPIC: _____ DATE: _____

Quote from Reading (pp._____) _____

HAPPINESS FOR ME

In his book *The Greatest Miracle in the World,* Og Mandino writes of the tremendous power that we have in our power of choice.... " Look at yourself. Think of the choices you have made in your life and recall, now, those bitter moments when you would fall on your knees if only you had the opportunity to choose again. What is past is past.... Use wisely your power of choice...."

We can think about the past—enjoying our happy memories or dwelling on our regrets. We can make plans for the future, but we can only live in the present. We must accept what we cannot change. We can grow from each mistake because we are capable of changing ourselves and becoming the person we want to be.

We all have done things that we regret, and wish that we could have another chance. There is the story of a mother who hurriedly took her toddler's special china cup out of her china cabinet to use at his birthday celebration. She dropped it in the process. The child wept as he clung to his mother. She wept as she clung to the broken pieces. Being human means being able to err. A broken dish is one thing. A heavy heart is another. The experience of hurting from a poor decision or error is an acknowledgment of sorrow. A good first step is to forgive one's self and to determine to take more positive actions.

Happiness—the choice is ours. It is up to us to determine our own answers as life questions us. We should look for the little things in life and appreciate the gifts of others as they touch our lives. We need to do those little things for others as our intuition prompts us to speak or lend a hand. So start now to develop an awareness of the happiness in life and share it with others. Life was meant to be enjoyed.

A student brought in a copy of Mandino's book *The Greatest Miracle in the World.* He suggested that the other students be encouraged to read it. "Tell them," he said "reading it will be a gift to themselves." Some of those who read it based their sharing on ideas taken from the book.

STUDENT DISCUSSION/ESSAY

"I'm happy when I have no anxieties. I believe what keeps me from being happy is my inability to accept a situation, usually an unhappy one," admitted a senior who opened the discussion on happiness. "I believe if I were given the chance to correct the past, I would do just that."

Jennifer spoke up, surprised that someone could feel as she did. "I feel the same. I find it hard to put a bad experience in the back of my mind. I think, what if I would have done this or said that, maybe the whole thing would not have happened. I did something that I regret and I wish so hard that I could go back and live it over. It's hard to accept the fact that nothing can be done about it. A good experience I can always share with a friend and think about it as a happy time. But a bad experience just sits there in my mind."

John was anxious to speak. "When people feel that they have done wrong, they need forgiveness. One time a friend confided to me that it was hard for him to believe that God could love him like his mom says he does. I told him that once you've done wrong, and had God take you back, then you'll believe it!"

Emily said: "I read Mandino's book and was surprised that an inspirational book could be fun to read. It is so easy to forget all the special aspects of our lives. We need to be reminded of the abundance of gifts with which we are endowed. We need to see that when they are used to help others, we become happier. It's really neat the way he writes."

Another student signaled to speak. "I liked the book, too, especially what he said about a person needing to have faith, courage, hope, and peace of mind, because these cause us to live and abide by our ideals and have faith in the future. People who lose faith in the future become unhappy."

Deanna read from her journal: "Og Mandino said some things that we all need to hear. I wish I could get my sister to read it. In particular, I found Og's *The Laws of Happiness and Success* applicable to my sister and me, as follows:

1) *Count your blessings.*
   Neither my sister nor I would have any trouble with this. My problem is that no matter how many I count, I will always be convinced that she has more. Yes, I am an envious younger sister, and I admit it.

2) *Proclaim your rarity.*
   I do this every time I write. I do it also when I admit my faults. I don't believe that my sister proclaims her rarity as often as she should. I must tell her that she certainly is a rare one.

3) *Go another mile.*
   This law is practically my theme. I make up for my lack of talent with effort. I work hard and I work for myself. My sister, on the other hand, seems to feel that because she is talented, people expect great things from her. She fears failure. I wish I could get her to work more for herself.

4) *Use wisely your power of choice.*
   This is a difficult one for both of us. We both realize that we have control over our lives. But how can we be sure that our decisions are wise? I often look to Billy Joel's song *James,* and I believe he meant that we must be true to ourselves or we will be living a lie."

Theresa, a serious young woman, made some rather astute observations about happiness: "There are different types of people: those who search for and find happiness: those who never search, but find it; and those who neither look for nor find anything. I want happiness in my life. I would like to be a person who stumbles upon it. But I won't be blind to anything new that comes along as I search for it."

Theresa paused and then continued, "There is usually joy in simple things and special people—children, the elderly, the mentally handicapped. They are so innocent and unaware of the terrible things around them."

Brian shared his first thought: "Happiness is when I get along with my family, because we fight sometimes and someone ends up getting hurt. We fight for stupid reasons, such as wearing each other's clothes."

Kathy, an intense, artistic student gave the assignment much thought. She read from her journal: "Happiness is related to others through friendship and love. If I have a friend, I am happy. If I'm sitting on a chair with my cat, Puffy, and I'm petting him and he's purring, I know that I love him and he loves me, which makes me happy. If I talk to a good looking boy, that makes me happy. If I listen to good music or write music or draw or write poetry, I am very happy."

Jesse shared his thinking: "To me happiness is having a life with a bare minimum of troubles. Happiness is contentment with what you have. Happiness is feeling something proud about one you love."

Kaitlin expressed the sentiments shared by many. She wrote: "Others and their well-being have a lot to do with my happiness. When people around me are happy, I am happy. Without other people I could not be happy, because through others I am able to give and to love. I'm happy when everything is going well, and when there is just the right amount of homework."

Ted, a conscientious young man, related his ideas to his part-time job. "My job involves high levels of happiness. I work after school with children and I reflect their happiness. My happiness is affected by the way others treat me. Happiness also deals with service. Volunteering helps me to be happy."

Molly held up an audio tape which she brought for her sharing. As she placed the tape into the recorder she explained: "I asked an elderly priest friend of mine if he would make a tape for our seminar on the subject of happiness. Father Jim is so crippled with arthritis that he can neither walk nor write, yet he is the happiest person I know. Looking back at life late in his life, he brings many thoughts into view.

> 'As a youngster, I didn't think I was supposed to be happy. I grew up in an atmosphere of feeling guilty. I was afraid to be happy because something bad might happen to compensate.
>
> 'Memories of my youth are happy, but I know that I wasn't happy. I would not let myself be happy. I worried all the time about things that would never develop. I remember thinking of a happiness as being too good to last. I thought other people could be happy, but I didn't think that it was in the realm of possibility for me to be happy.
>
> 'I remember needing specifics to be happy. I was never satisfied and wished things were different. I had time, place, and people requirements. Happiness was saved for the weekends or for special moments. Young people, at least in my generation, were so unaware that they were happy when they were laughing with friends or going places.
>
> 'It wasn't until later in my life at a rehabilitation center for alcoholics that I realized that my happiness was my own responsibility. I became aware that happiness was an attitude toward life. I learned that happiness was not having what I want, but wanting what I have. I realized that I, as an individual, had a choice. I have a choice every moment of every day. I can choose to be happy, to worry, to be anxious, to be afraid, or not to be. It's up to me.'"

Student responses to Father Jim's thoughts were spontaneous. Kevin said, "He made me realize things about life that I hadn't thought of before—like never being satisfied and wishing things could be different."

"I really felt he was talking to me when he said that we shouldn't be thinking of the *if's* needed to make us happy," Bernadette responded.

"I thought what he said was inspirational. It makes me realize that I should look hard into my life and be happy now with the things that I experience."

"It is I who decides whether or not I am to be happy. I liked that statement," Whitney added.

Elise remarked, "Put another way, it says, I am responsible for my own happiness! That means that I can't wait for happiness to come, but I have to make it happen."

"I'm still thinking about that statement, too. I never really thought much about happiness before, other than I want to be happy. Now I must realize that my happiness is up to me. I can't depend on anyone else to make me happy." Stephanie sounded unsure.

Rob put in, "That statement isn't any heavier than his saying that you shouldn't worry about what you want, but want what you have!"

Peggy raised her hand. "I liked that, too. Now I can understand how the poor can be happy. They can choose to be happy. They are able to accept what they cannot change. Father Jim is talking about an attitude toward life."

Michelle countered, "You agree with Father Jim that happiness is an attitude? I believe that happiness is something inside. If you're not happy inside, nothing will make you happy. I am happy with friends, because I have a good time. I am happy that my family is healthy, because it makes me feel secure. I am happy when I get good grades, because it makes me feel proud. If I were not happy with myself inside, I would not feel secure or proud or happy."

Pablo asked, "Isn't that something inside your attitude toward life and yourself, Michelle?"

Christopher joined in the conversation. "What Father Jim says ties in with Og Mandino's fourth *Law of Happiness and Success*. I liked it so well that I copied it into my journal:

'Use wisely your power of choice:
Choose to love…rather than hate.
Choose to laugh…rather than cry.
Choose to create…rather than destroy.
Choose to persevere…rather than quit.
Choose to praise…rather than gossip.
Choose to heal…rather than wound.
Choose to give…rather than steal.
Choose to act…rather than procrastinate.
Choose to grow…rather that rot.
Choose to pray…rather than curse.
Choose to live…rather than die.'"

"Maybe one's definition of happiness changes as a person gets older," Becky said thoughtfully. "My mother said that she's happy when her children are happy."

Objectives: *To recognize I am responsible for my own happiness* *To acknowledge that happiness is a choice*   EXERCISE/JOURNAL SHEET

HAPPINESS FOR ME

1. Comment on *The Laws of Happiness and Success* by Og Mandino:

    a. *Count your blessings.*

    b. *Proclaim your rarity.*

    c. *Go another mile.*

    c. *Use wisely the power of choice.*

2. How will choosing to be happy change your life?

3. What does accepting the responsibility for your own life mean to you?

4. How can you make happiness happen? Explain.

WRITE A SHORT ESSAY on one of the topics or CHOOSE A QUOTE from the readings. Cite an example. Relate it to yourself or to someone you know.

TOPIC: _____ DATE: _____

Quote from Reading (pp._____) _____

14 THE JOYS OF LIVING

OBJECTIVES:

1. To appreciate my humanity
2. To acknowledge even a trifling joy
3. To recall a single kindness
4. To share our reflections on faith, hope, dignity, and the value of suffering
5. To discover the meaning of saying yes to life

Remembering

Who but you
would ever do
the little things
that speak so true
and make a heart
so very full —
remembering
is
beautiful.

THESE THINGS I REMEMBER

In *Man's Search for Meaning*, Viktor Frankl's account of life in a Nazi prison camp, he recalls that even in such dire circumstances there was evidence of joy in the most simple things that spoke of love, friendship, and dignity.

To create an awareness of this joy experienced in the little things of life, we can think back in our own lives, or lives we have witnessed, and cite an example for each of the following: a trifling joy, a single kindness, an expression of hope, an act of faith, an example of dignity, and of the value in suffering.

We remember those things that strike us emotionally. Often we can recall an incident from childhood as if it happened yesterday.

A trifling joy
This may be something trivial that someone did for us, or something special that someone said that held meaning for us.

A single kindness
Human beings are so fragile. Sometimes, when the burdens of life are heavy, a single kindness can lift our hearts and brighten our day. It is also important to realize the gifts of our person, and their power for good in the lives of others.

An expression of hope
Every positive action we perform, every volunteer hour we spend, every smile that we give, every word of cheer that we offer, every prayer that we say, every act of kindness we do, causes hope to arise in someone's heart.

An act of faith
—is witness to one's belief. Faith is a gift that is earned by us in experiencing life. Unlike love, which is freely given, faith cannot be taken away.

Dignity
—is pride in being. Frankl refers to dignity as a choice. It is "the last of the human freedoms—to choose one's attitude in any given set of circumstances, to choose one's own way."

Suffering has value
—when we accept what we cannot change. Spinoza, a German philosopher, wrote in his book entitled *Ethics,* "Emotion, which is suffering, ceases to be suffering as soon as we form a clear and precise picture of it."

There are many ways to learn, and none better than by example. Sometimes we learn from the example set by an older person; other times we learn from the goodness of a child.

Warm smiles are often seen as we recount particular incidents that hold meaning for us. These sharings of seemingly trivial moments are often etched in our memories.

STUDENT DISCUSSION/ESSAY

A trifling joy

Ron was anxious to speak first. "I remember being in the sixth grade and hurrying home from school to find out what my baby sister had done that day.

"My mom found out that she was pregnant just when she was going to start nurse's training," he continued. "My dad told her that if she would have the baby, he would change shifts at work so he could take care of the baby while she went to school. He did.

"One day dad said that he couldn't find Mandy. Then he heard noises from the bottom cupboard. There she was with the pots and pans." Ron had so much pride and joy in his family that he spoke of them often.

"When I was little, I found a stray dog in my yard. In the few minutes that I played with him, I experienced a great feeling of joy," Rick admitted with a grin.

"Mine? The first time someone kissed me other than a relative, and yes, I remember her name." David was blushing from his admission.

Then Jolie spoke, though careful not to reveal who had given her joy: "When I was really down because I was having a bad day, this person came up and gave me a big hug."

"I coached a volleyball team for sixth grade girls, when I was a freshman," Kim related. "I worked them very hard and taught them things that sixth graders usually don't learn about the game. They respected me, but they always complained about how hard they had to work. Well, they won the league championship. Afterwards, they thanked me, apologized for their complaining, and asked me to coach them again the next year." Kim was brimming with pride as she told of the experience.

"When I was a sophomore, a senior helped me with my equipment and some plays during football practice," a senior athlete recalled. Someone special, whom he had admired, noticed him, helped him. A memory was made.

"The first time I put my hand in the catcher's mitt here at school, I thought of Frank Stams and other great athletes who had used that glove!" Tom admitted with enthusiasm.

"I remember my uncle buying a whole garbage bag full of candy for our reunion!" John's voice was full of wonder and surprise, just as he must have been when it happened.

"My parents went out of their way to attend a concert in which I was playing," Jennifer said with pride.

A single kindness

Lisa, a vibrant outgoing young woman, raised her hand to open the discussion. "I work for a fast-food chicken chain. They're closed for Thanksgiving Day. So I asked my boss if I could come in and do six chickens to take to two needy families. He not only agreed but he added to the menu. When we delivered the food, the families were so happy, so grateful. They had so little, yet they invited us to eat with them. It was hard to say no and not offend them."

Cassie was next to speak: "Yours was a big kindness, Lisa. Mine is more trivial, but memorable. I forgot my lunch on game day, and we were leaving school early. I only had a quarter. A friend gave me her lunch." Cassie smiled at Lisa after her admission.

"A stranger cared for me when I was hurt. Now he is a good friend. His name is Damien."

"Last year my friends thought that I had *anorexia nervosa* and tried to help me. They cared about me." Andrea had obviously been touched by their kindness.

"I did a kindness by being with a friend after her grandfather died. Just my being there at

183

that time seemed to help her, and made me feel good, too," Amy said.

Matt told of the daily example of hope that he witnesses in his mother. "My brother, Danny, has been in a coma for two years, but Mom still prays for him every night."

"Every sunrise, every new spring, every time I stop and appreciate the beauty that exists amid the pain and sorrow of life, speaks to me of hope," Theresa said thoughtfully.

"I know two little boys who are best friends. One boy, Joey, received a small toy truck for Christmas that his friend admired. Joey gave the truck to his friend. This incident spoke of hope to me," Tim offered.

"Yeah! Children! I see hope each day watching and working with latch-key children after school," Troy agreed. "Children are our future."

"Encouraging a friend in doubt, as someone did for me," put in Kate, softly.

"Church and the coming of the Lord," voiced another.

"A tiny baby's cry," Sara added.

"I think that I show my faith in God when I have faith in other people—those I love, or those I don't even know," Connie explained.

"My parents were having serious problems. I was brought in to it," Michelle began. "I was pulled from both sides and from within. I didn't know what to do anymore, so I told God that I was putting my problems into His hands. He took care of me. I was able to face everything that we went through without a doubt in my mind."

"I was asked to be a godmother," Missy said proudly.

"My grandma has great faith. I always like it when she says she prays for me." Darin was proud.

Christopher, a bright, sincere, young man wrote this essay in his journal: "Nature is my favorite way to find God. Not long ago, I took a walk on a bitterly cold, windy night. A heavy cover of fresh snow muffled most noises of traffic. The clouds raced across the sky, breaking here and there, revealing myriad patterns of diamond-like stars. The wind blew eerily through the trees. It was just me, the wind, the stars, and the earth. I felt in tune with the universe, a part of it rather than an inhabitant of it. I felt closer to God than I ever had. I thanked Him for allowing me to be alive that night to experience the wind and the cold, to experience Him."

Dignity

A young man cited an incident he had seen on TV about World War II: "A Nazi soldier pressed his cane against an old woman's throat so that she had to look up at him. The old woman said nothing, but I could sense that nothing the Nazi would do to her could actually take away her dignity as a person."

Shelly followed, saying, "My dad taught me the importance of self-respect. He said that I should only do things that would bring pride and dignity to the family."

A quiet, young man spoke up. "Once I kept my cool when others were egging me on."

"My dad works so hard and takes such pride in what he does. Even though I get upset with him sometimes, he is a great father. He taught me the importance of thinking positive," Angela related.

"My brother nearly destroyed our family because he was on drugs. But my family had dignity. We stuck together, and we made it."

"When someone gets on my nerves really bad, I want to tell him off, but I let it slide." Scott let his voice fall with his admission.

"Dignity to me is being able to say no to certain things to preserve my self-worth," put in another young man.

In her essay, a young woman wrote: "Dignity is often witnessed in the elderly as they accept their human condition and await in hope the angel of death. I saw this in my grandmother. In her final days my grandma spoke joyously of the angel's coming for her. Her attitude in itself was her final gift to our family."

Suffering has value

> God wants us all to love Him
> Every moment of each day.
> Of each He asks an offering—
> Something of the heart's bouquet.
> Some of us were made to toil,
> While others were made to play.
> Of some He asks for patience,
> Of some a lonely day.
> Some must give of their heartache,
> Others must share of their pain . . .
> Each of us can add our prayer
> That in glory He might reign.
> The children bring their laughter,
> Like the lilybells of spring;
> Teenagers add their hearts of love
> And all of the songs they sing.
> No one knows how great a share
> The least of us can impart,
> For the beauty is measured as
> God reads from each one's heart.
> By the beauty of our lives,
> We bear witness to our love,
> For the tapestry we weave
> Is our prayer to God above.

In his essay a young man wrote: "When they had the cutbacks at my uncle's company, my Uncle Jack was laid off. He had had a very good job. It all happened suddenly. My Aunt May, Mom's sister, was worried about him. She knew that he could get another job, but having been 'let go' took the spirit right out of him. That was two years ago. Aunt May was right—he got another job, and in time, he got his spirit back, and I wondered how. We talked, and I asked him. But first, I told him about not being named a captain on the football team, which I had worked so hard for and wanted so badly. I told him that when my name was missing from those posted on the list, I had thought of him—of how he must have felt when the spirit was taken right out of him. Uncle Jack told me that it happened at a summer concert, when Benjamin Britten's *War Requiem* was sung. He said that as he read the offertory, the words '. . . offer pride as sacrifice . . .' seemed meant for him. In that moment he realized that pride was the cause of his suffering. When he accepted it, his spirit for life came back. So did mine, when I realized that pride got in my way."

Objectives: *To appreciate my humanity*
To acknowledge a trifling joy
To recall a single kindness
To share reflections of hope, dignity, faith, and value in suffering

EXERCISE/JOURNAL SHEET

THESE THINGS I REMEMBER

A *trifling joy*—something trivial but memorable that someone did for you, or something special that someone said that held meaning for you. Include who, what, and when.

A *single kindness*—something someone did for you, or a kindness that you did for someone else.

AND I REMEMBER THESE, TOO

You will have to think a little harder, perhaps, to recall an example of an expression of hope, of dignity, of faith as witness to your belief; and the value of suffering and accepting that which cannot be changed.

Recall an incident when you:

1. Offered someone an expression of hope.

2. Maintained your dignity, or helped someone else maintain his or hers.

3. Witnessed to your faith.

4. Were able to accept suffering or unhappiness that came your way.

WRITE A SHORT ESSAY on one of the topics or CHOOSE A QUOTE from the readings. Relate it to yourself or to someone you know. Cite an example.

TOPIC: _____ DATE: _____

Quote from Reading (pp._____) _____

SAY YES TO LIFE

One day a vivacious young woman came to the seminar with an experience to share: "When I got home from school yesterday, my neighbors called and asked if I would help them find their missing puppies. I had other plans, but I agreed. Their dog, Bowzer, had a litter of five golden retrievers, and all five of the week-old pups had gotten away. As we searched for them, we talked. I hadn't really seen much of them in the past few years. They were in college now. We made plans to go out together. By dinner time it was dark, and we had found four of the puppies. The next morning, when I was leaving for school, the fifth puppy was on our front stoop! Is that what saying yes to life means?"

Melissa had accepted a challenge and followed it through, thus saying yes to life.

Another way to discover what is meant by saying yes to life is to take one day and make an honest effort to establish as many positive attitudes and actions as possible.

We have the power to change the world. By what we are and by all that we do, we affect the lives of others. The more goodness that we share with others, the greater joy we have in our own hearts.

STUDENT DISCUSSION/ESSAY

A happy, mature young woman said, "I have learned that the placing of a smile on my face will not only make me feel better, but will make others feel more at ease around me. I work in a restaurant. When I'm in a bad mood I don't smile, and I feel distant from the customers. When I wear a smile, the people are comfortable and easier to get along with, and I feel as though I am a part of them. Many close friendships have resulted."

Paul, a self-assured young man, offered another example of how the actions of one person can affect other people. "Yesterday, I had a bad day, and I acted exactly like someone who was having a bad day. I am sure that I put dampers on others by blowing off steam. I know for a fact that I find it easier to get through a day if the problems of the person next to me stay with that person. Yet, I didn't extend that courtesy to others."

In her essay, Sally talks about her work on a service project. "I went with my youth group from church to help the poor in Appalachia. The experience that I gained there changed me forever. Bringing sunshine into the house of an elderly lady, and seeing the smile on her face, changed me. The experiences that I had with those friends will always be remembered because they made us spiritually close."

Charles agreed to read what he discovered when he chose one day and filled it with positive actions:

SAY YES TO LIFE

ATTITUDE/ACTION	WHO/WHAT	REACTION	EFFECT ON ME
Speak to all you meet.	A "hello" to everyone.	"Hello" back; some talked.	Nice.
Make positive statements.	To girlfriend: "You look pretty."	"Oh yeah? I just threw this on."	I felt insulted.
Do a favor.	Loaned friend lunch money.	Thankful.	Glad I helped.
Walk to class different way.		Saw other friends.	Pleasant stroll.
Do something for someone.	Babysat for neighbor.	Grateful.	Enjoyed helping.
Share beauty with someone.	Went to river with my girl.	Pretty scenery.	I thought it was romantic.
Make eye contact when speaking.	Friends/strangers	Returned eye contact.	Felt confident.
Ask a favor.	Ride home/friend.	No problem.	Appreciated it.
Return a phone call.	Friend/ long distance.	Surprised, glad.	I missed him. He listened.
Give a compliment.	Always do to friends/family.	Some like it; some shrugged.	I liked doing it.
Write a note.	Friend at college.	Happy/wrote back.	Felt good.
Say "I love you."	My mom.	She was happy.	Made me happy.
Mend a heart.	Made up with Mom/argument.	She was surprised.	Both felt happy.
Visit to church.	Prayed.	Thankful to God.	Felt good.
Be creative.	Made birthday card/sister.	She really liked it.	I felt good.
Put on a happy face.	Smiled at everyone.	Positive responses.	Put me in good mood.

Charles summed up his reaction to his positive day, saying, "My friend started laughing and said, 'Every time I see you, you're smiling.' So I laughed, too. He had noticed. I was really glad to brighten other peoples' day. It was a good experience for me, too."

Objective: To discover the meaning of saying yes to life EXERCISE/JOURNAL SHEET

SAY YES TO LIFE

Choose a week, and during that week try to include all of the actions described below:

ATTITUDE/ACTION	WHO/WHAT	REACTION	EFFECT ON ME
Speak to all you meet.			
Pay a compliment.			
Do a favor.			
Walk a different way to class.			

ATTITUDE/ACTION	WHO/WHAT	REACTION	EFFECT ON ME
Do something for someone.			
Share beauty with someone.			
Make eye contact when speaking.			
Return a phone call.			
Tell someone, "I love you."			
Make a date with a friend.			

ATTITUDE/ACTION	WHO/WHAT	REACTION	EFFECT ON ME
Mend a heart.			
Be creative.			
Write a note.			
Volunteer.			
Other.			

WRITE A SHORT ESSAY on one of the topics below:

1. What was your reaction to this positive experience?

2. Recall an occasion when you accepted a challenge for a positive action. Include the action: for whom? what? Give the reactions noted in yourself/other(s).

TOPIC: _____ DATE: _____

15 SUCCESS IN MY LIFE

OBJECTIVES:

1. To consider how other people define success
2. To define the meaning of success for myself
3. To recognize choosing a mate as an important decision
4. To share ideas and ideals related to a happy marriage

> "To laugh often and much; to win the respect of intelligent people and the affection of children; to earn the appreciation of honest critics and endure the betrayal of false friends; to appreciate beauty; to find the best in others; to leave the world a bit better, whether by a healthy child, a garden patch or a redeemed social condition; to know even one life has breathed easier because you lived. This is to have succeeded."
> —Harry Emerson Fosdick

WHAT IS SUCCESS?

What has the meaning of success become that its price causes so much stress in us today?

What is the measure of success? Is it money, material goods, power, prestige? Yes, most assuredly all of these, in a worldly sense, and that can't be denied. We all strive for some of these things in our lives. Success can mean many things; it is different things to different people.

We base our definitions of success on our own personal goals. Sometimes stress stems in part from the goals our parents hold for us versus the personal goals we have set for ourselves. We mature by being responsible for our own choices. The goals we set for ourselves determine how we will live our lives.

Often children misinterpret parental prodding for them to excel in all levels of endeavor. Most parents equate their own success with the happiness they desire for their children. Most parents are unselfish. They want their children to do their best and to be their best so that they and their families to come can enjoy the fruits of life.

We need to set parameters in defining *success*. We need to affirm certain truths: that success needs to be earned; that we need to do our best work; and that we should develop and use our talents. By meeting these conditions we will take pride in our work and will have a feeling of satisfaction in a job well done. Ultimately, happiness will be ours in the knowledge of a victory achieved from within—from the heart. Those who define *success* in this way may choose to pursue careers such as: builder, architect, artisan, artist, surgeon, physical or speech therapist, florist, and the like—those who can see the work of their hands.

Some may define *success* as making other people happy by helping them to reach their goals. This philanthropic approach to life suggests career choices such as: teacher, minister, social worker, counselor, nurse, doctor, or missionary.

Success can come even through small goals that one has striven for on a daily basis. Recognizing these minor achievements in a complimentary way encourages further development. Joy comes in the knowledge of fulfillment, and is not measured by the size of the goal.

The Nobel Peace Prize recognizes persons whose efforts have most benefited mankind. A person receiving this award is internationally acclaimed as "successful" in that field. Included in a recent list of these outstanding individuals were doctors, scientists, authors, and a nun working with the "poorest of the poor" on the streets of Calcutta, India.

STUDENT DISCUSSION/ESSAY

A young woman wrote in her journal: "I think the main cause of most my stress is my parents, and my going to college. I worry about letting them down, so I have extra pressure to excel, to get ahead, to be a success. Sometimes I think it's more important to please myself, but I feel obligated to make my parents proud of me."

A young man wrote: "Stress is caused by most everything that I do in life. Most of my stress is caused by my parents. They are always pushing me to do the right thing and get good grades, to make something of myself. I am stressed by everything whether it is playing in a basketball game or taking a test."

Philip, a diligent young man, reports on surveying his parents' responses to the meaning of success, and adds his own remarks, saying: "To my father, success is being Number One and being a winner. However, after thinking about it for a moment, my father stated that success is accomplishing what you want to with your life. He quoted Teddy Roosevelt: 'There is no success unless you have tried.' My mother said that having good children, who make their way in life, and are happy and content would fulfill her purpose in life. This would be her success. My personal definition of success is getting the most that one can out of life. I feel that people are a success if they put forth their best effort in everything they do. Likewise, being spiritually, mentally, physically, and emotionally strong makes one a success. If people learn from their mistakes, they are succeeding. However, being Number One does not make one a success, if the person does not work long and hard to achieve it. John Powell, in *Free To Be Me*, states that most of us use only ten percent of our human potential.

Jennifer, a vivacious teen, said: "My dad thinks of success as happiness and satisfaction in what you have done, and pride in your work. I agree with him, but I would stress happiness. I won't think of myself as successful unless I'm happy. Some people value their economic well-being rather than their personal happiness."

Stephanie responded, "I agree that success is meeting your goals, when you have worked for them. But people are rarely satisfied, so success seems so hard to reach. For me success is knowing that I've made others happy, and have helped them to reach their goals. Sometimes, people equate success with happiness, but that's not always true. A person can be successful and not be happy, but one can be happy in life without necessarily being successful in other people's eyes."

Todd, a quiet teen, offered: "I asked my grandfather the meaning of *success*. He told me that success means being the best you can be. You don't have to be a superstar or rich to be successful. It's the way you work in life. If you work to be the best you can, then in your heart you know you are successful. To be a success means being able to look back at life and know you have accomplished your goals."

"I agree with Stephanie," put in Anne. "Success to me is helping other people and seeing them benefit from my help. If people are wealthy, it has no meaning if they cannot share it or help someone less fortunate. To my parents, success is watching their children grow and mature, and eventually become active members of the community. The actions we show, such as leadership and responsibility, reflect the lessons they taught us."

Tony, a paradox of physical strength, whimsical humor, and spiritual depth, stated: "I feel success means setting goals for yourself and achieving those goals. Some people feel that success is monetary, but not necessarily. It could be anything from losing weight to getting the job you've always wanted. Success is very life-fulfilling. I know this is true because all people feel this way. When did you ever hear of people looking back with pride or pleasure at their failures? They like to look back at their successes, not their failures. Success is a universal feeling of accomplishment."

After hearing all the definitions of what makes for success, the group came up with the following summary:

Success is
- making a friend
- a job well done
- a happy marriage
- giving birth to a baby
- raising a child
  - listening to and encouraging them
  - being there for them
- overcoming loneliness caused by
  - a misunderstanding
  - a new direction in life
  - the loss of a friend
  - moving to a new area
  - starting a new job
- conquering the fear
  - of sleepless nights
  - of being accepted
  - of trying something new
  - of taking a test
  - of trying a new food
  - of the future
- meeting the challenge
  - of making a team
  - of winning a race
  - of getting a job
  - of speaking out
  - of saying no to peer pressure
- taking the risk
  - of saying hello
  - of making a date
  - of offering an opinion
  - of asking a question
  - of volunteering
  - of being different
  - of saying yes to life
- learning
  - to accept what can't be changed
  - to be tolerant
  - to be true to oneself
  - to play the piano
  - to reach a high note
- being happy
  - with who you are
  - with what you have
- taking a journey inward
  - to know one's self
  - to accept one's self
- And finally, success is having lived so that our death will be
  - a tribute to a life well lived
  - a God well loved

Objectives: *To consider how other people define success* EXERCISE/JOURNAL SHEET
To define success for one's self

WHAT IS SUCCESS?

Survey Questions:

1. Complete the statement: Success is _____

   _____

   (in terms of the little things that you have worked hard to achieve).

2. Ask the following people to define *success:*

   a. Your parent(s)

   b. Your grandparent(s)

   c. An admired adult

   d. A child

WRITE A SHORT ESSAY related to one of the definitions above or CHOOSE A QUOTE from the readings. Cite an example. Relate it to yourself or someone you know.

TOPIC: _____ DATE: _____

Quote from Reading (pp.____) _____

THE PERSON I WILL MARRY

A successful life in many respects will be determined by the person we choose to marry. The choice of our mate is the most important decision we make in life, if we marry. The person we marry will help to decide where we will live, and how we will live. To a great extent it will determine if we will have the privilege of being ourselves—appreciated for who we are, encouraged to share the gifts of our talents, and thus become the best we can be. Or one partner may cause the other to compromise to meet his or her needs and/or the needs of others.

People marry for many reasons, a true love commitment being the most prized. Love at first sight happens, but it is the exception to the rule. Choosing a marriage partner is often dependent upon our feelings of self, and/or our goals in life. Not everyone finds his or her own true love. Sometimes men and women are drawn into marriage by mutual admiration, a desire to overcome loneliness, a desire for their own home and a family. Often these are very sound marriages.

Marriage should, of course, not be entered into lightly. It should be a commitment to love and honor each other—a sacrament most holy. A good marriage is the basic building block to which our society and civilization are anchored. A happy marriage is the source of joy for a happy child, a source of pride and direction for the growing youth. A happy marriage is the hope and mainstay of the next generation, the firmest basis for good public opinion, and the surest wealth of a nation.

The strongest part of any human relationship is the ability to talk openly to one another. We should feel free to communicate personal feelings on how we look at life. We should speak of aspirations and of deep commitments, thereby sharing a pride in one another. We should welcome the sharing of the other's humor, pathos, and philosophy of life. In considering a marriage commitment the couple should discuss their financial situations and share their views on having or not having children.

It is important to get to know the family of our intended. A marriage can bring a family closer or may alienate them completely. Getting to know each other's family, gives us an insight as to whether or not we will "fit in" with them.

Success in marriage, as in other aspects of life, just doesn't happen. Each person must work toward its success; work toward its fulfillment; work to make the other happy; appreciate each other.

STUDENT DISCUSSION/ESSAY

Angela opened the discussion. "My parents' marriage was arranged. My mother says that she grew to love my dad and cannot imagine having married anyone else."

A young man spoke out, "My uncle had a good marriage as long as he had a job. When his job was cut, his wife left him and married someone else. I'm looking for commitment."

A self-assured student expressed the desire to seek her career first. This young woman had a zest for living and often spoke out frankly. "I know what I want, and I will work hard to achieve it. I want a good job and a nice apartment. I don't know about marriage and a family. I've seen my mother get dumped on by my dad and older brothers. It's 'get this and do that.' I'm not going to be a step-and-fetch-it!"

A mature senior man made a single statement concerning his quest for his future bride: "I want a woman who will be of one mind with me."

A young man who had seemed only preoccupied with rebuilding his car said, "If I could find a girl who could love me, just for me, I would never talk about cars again."

When it was Bridget's turn she spoke directly saying, "I want the promise of a lasting marriage. No divorce!"

Jane addressed the strengths she witnessed in her parents' marriage. "Christian faith and values are of great importance to my parents. I know this is true, because they both work and sacrifice for us. Family closeness is also prized."

Larry said, "My parents are tolerant. My mother takes us to church every Sunday with our grandparents; my father never goes. Dad's relatives do not attend any church. None of my relatives ever mentions this difference, although they all have known each other since my parents were children."

Nancy smiled as she offered, "Mutual respect and good manners are important to my parents. No smoking or rude language is permitted in our house, and they never say or do anything hurtful."

Colleen shared values that she had known in her parents' marriage: "My mom and dad are able to tough out bad times by working together and trusting in God's help."

Jo offered, "When I asked my mom what she would look for in the person I marry, she said, 'Someone who is exciting to you, and with whom there is an appreciation of each other's intrinsic worth and integrity.'"

Kaitlin waved a paper she was holding in her hand. She said, "My older sister is to be married next month and she received this letter from her mother-in-law-to-be. She said that I could share it with you. I'll just read part, so you can see how lucky my sister is. . . . 'It's only been lately, as your wedding day draws nearer, that I've begun to think of you as a person in your own right, instead of just my son's future wife. Now I find myself hoping that he'll measure up and make you a good husband. . . . His dad has tried, by example, to give him the right sense of values and to teach him to recognize his duties and responsibilities. I've tried to teach him to believe in God, love his fellow man, and not be ashamed to live by a decent code of morals. Between us, we have tried to make him gentle when gentleness is called for and tough and unafraid when courage and strength are needed. I hope, for your sake, that our teachings have taken root. You see, I want him to be the kind of a husband a girl like you deserves. . . . When your father gives you to my son in the wedding ceremony so I, too, will be giving my son into your keeping—to have and to hold until death do you part. I'll do it gladly with no apron strings attached and only a deep love in my heart for both of you.'"

"Wow! I hope that I will be so lucky!" someone whispered aloud.

In his essay a young man wrote, "I don't think my parents' marriage could have weathered the trauma of job instability and my father's neuroses without the strong sense of responsibility engendered by family traditions and religious beliefs. The dependence of us children, initially, and more recently our support have been important factors."

In addressing the statement that choosing a marriage partner is the most import decision in our life, a young woman wrote: "...you commit the rest of your life to the person you marry. Together you share both happy and sad times. Hopefully, you will have children, and you need to rear them in an atmosphere of love and warmth. In marriage, two people must learn to sacrifice and compromise. Marriage is a challenge, but it can be successful if both persons put everything they have into it."

A quiet, gentle, senior woman wrote: "When I love someone, I try to be whatever they need me to be. If they are upset, I am there to listen to them and to try to help. When they are happy and celebrating, I am by their side celebrating with them. I hope when I marry, my husband will understand this meaning of 'I love you' and will try to be what I need him to be. If we work together helping each other our relationship should last forever."

A young man put much thought into his essay as he wrote of love: "...Love deals with two people—myself and the other person. I not only feel a closeness, but also a desire to share and to give of myself to the other person. Love is a commitment. A commitment means that we chose to do something and we must adhere to it.... Love is like a flower. It is a seed that is planted within us. It must be accepted by us and nurtured in order that it may grow. When it grows, it blossoms into something that is beautiful.... If this flower is left unnurtured, it cannot survive. So it is with our love. We must commit to each other unconditionally, and our love will be strong and growing."

Objectives: *To recognize choosing a marriage partner is*
the most important decision in our life
To share ideas and ideals related to a happy marriage

EXERCISE/JOURNAL SHEET

THE PERSON I WILL MARRY

SURVEY QUESTION: What makes for a happy marriage?

Ask two married people (or two married couples) you know.

    Person (relationship to you)   Criterion

1. _____   _____

2. _____   _____

Name three things parents might look for in the person you marry.

1. _____

2. _____

3. _____

List three things that you think are important in your parents' marriage. Why do you think they are important?

1. _____

2. _____

3. _____

What are three things that you will look for in the person you marry?

1. _____

2. _____

3. _____

WRITE A SHORT ESSAY on one of the topics, or write on: Marriage partner—the most important decision in my life.

TOPIC: _____ DATE: _____

16 THE FINAL SHARING

OBJECTIVES:

1. For each of us to share with the seminar something that is important to us
   - an idea
   - a creative work
   - a talent
   - a witness to faith
   - family
   - personal philosophy of life
   - other
2. To let other students get to know us better

THE FINAL SHARING

At the semester's end the students, individually, are asked to take five or ten minutes and share with the others something about themselves. They are told about this in advance and the following suggestions are made: The sharing can be a short talk on any subject you choose that is of importance to you; for example, it could be about your family; it might be about something or someone that has been influential in helping to shape your life. Or you may choose to share with the others a special talent or artistic gift you have: a portfolio of art, a vocal or instrumental solo, some needlework, a dance, an original piece of writing, a poem.

One young man confided to me that all of his reflections on who had been the most important influence in his life had one single answer: his grandmother. He wondered if he would be able to fully communicate to his classmates the sense of pride and joy she had instilled in him and the support he had received from his early childhood up to the present. While he was assembling his thoughts and feelings into an outline for his sharing, it suddenly struck him: the best way he could show his friends how the magnitude of his grandmother's gifts had influenced him was to carry into fruition the promise she had seen in him. He would certainly try! His was a memorable sharing that final day of the seminar.

STUDENT DISCUSSION

Jim began the final sharings. From his gym bag he pulled out, one at a time, the framed senior photos of his five older brothers. He had taken them from the fireplace mantel and placed them in order, oldest to youngest, into his canvas bag. Jim introduced each brother to the class as he held up their photograph.

"This is Joe, my oldest brother. He's got a good job. He's married and has three kids.

"This is Frank. He's not married. He sells used cars and does pretty well. In fact, if it weren't for Frank sending my brother Mike money each month for food, I don't think Mike could afford to stay at Ohio State.

"Here's Mike. He weighed 235 pounds as a senior here before he got his scholarship to play football at OSU.

"This is Pat. He's the student of the family. He wants to be a lawyer.

And this is Tony. He graduated last year. Remember him? He played the line, too, but wasn't as big as Mike.

Then there's me. I didn't bring my photo because you see me every day. My grades are good but, like Tony, I'm undecided about what to do with my life. I have another brother, Angelo, who is still in grade school. Oh, and I have two younger sisters."

As he placed the framed photographs back into his gym bag, there was much applause. It was evident that Jim was proud of his family. The students had a better picture of Jim as a person, knowing something about his family.

Eileen's final sharing was a kind of "show and tell." "I want to tell you about a hobby which I have shared with my grandmother—quilt making," she said as she took from a large plastic bag a full-sized green and white quilt. "With Grandma's help I have made five bed quilts. Because of their size I only brought in one to show you. However, I did bring in photographs of the other four. First, I would like to explain to you a little bit about quilting. It is the art of stitching two or more thicknesses of fabric together in a planned design. Lightweight padding is stitched to the underside of the fabric to produce a puffed effect, as you see in the geometric designs on this quilt. Using a Quilter Foot, which is a tool that attaches to the sewing machine, the stitching of the padded fabric is simplified. In this photo of my floral quilt, you can see that the design was in the fabric itself. I stitched around the flowers with the quilter. This next photo is of a quilt made out of my father's and brothers' silk ties. It took a lot of cutting and piecing to make this quilt." Eileen answered many questions and let her peers examine the green and white quilt and the photos of the others. The students were genuinely pleased with her presentation.

Margaret, a pretty varsity athlete, shared an incident about the nursing home where she worked after school: "Mrs. M, a patient whom I feed, was so weak that night that she struggled to swallow jello. I went to the floor nurse and told her of her condition, saying, 'Perhaps you should take a look at her.' The nurse answered, 'No, Mrs. M is weak, but she is fine. Now go along and see how much you can get her to eat.'"

Margaret caught her breath and continued: "The following day, Mrs. M was no better. She had her eyes closed most of the time and showed no interest in eating. Again, I reported to the floor nurse, and again was told to do what I could for her and not to worry.

"On the third day, when I entered her room," recalled Margaret, "she was ashen and lying so still that I thought she was dead. I hastened to take her pulse. It was very weak. I wondered what to do. I had her tray. 'Perhaps, if I were to raise her head and offer her a little broth?' I thought. Gently, I slid my hand under her head, and balancing a spoonful of broth in my other hand brought it to her lips. Her teeth were clenched. The broth dribbled down from her lips. For a moment I froze. Then I quickly checked her pulse: 'No pulse! Oh God!' I thought, 'she's dead!'

"I ran out to the front desk for help. The floor nurse came with me to check her. 'No pulse,' she confirmed. 'You're right. Mrs. M is dead. Bathe the corpse.'

"Bathe the corpse? I was dumbfounded. I turned to tell the nurse no, but she was gone. There I was with the body. I was so frightened. I wanted to run away. I was shaking. What to do? As I turned to look at Mrs. M, I became aware that she had died in my presence. I couldn't just leave her. Then something unusual happened to me. As I gently bathed her, a sense of peace came over me. It was like her gift to me. I shall never forget this experience."

"Wow!" seemed to be the expression on the face of each student. There was silence, and then a thunderous applause. Margaret had shared something from the heart, a gift she had received of courage and love.

A young man, smiling broadly, set a small, portable CD player on the front desk and turned to speak: "My name is Thomas-Edward-Allan-Joseph-Marcus-William-Peter-James-John-Gerald-Kevin-Randall-David-Timothy-Paul Kraft. Tom for short. Many of you have thought of me as the class clown. In many instances that has been true, because I didn't know if you would accept the other side of me—my serious side. Today I will present to you selections from my verse." Tom turned on his CD player and adjusted the volume, then in a very composed manner began to read his first to a background of music:

Who Am I?

Who am I?
A blooming rose?
Living my life
in which
anything goes?
Concerned individual?
Gentle and kind?
I keep searching myself
to learn what I'll find?
I've found quite a lot,
but it's not enough.
I still have to find
my true basic stuff.
But who am I really?
How will I know
just what makes me tick
or what makes me go?
I'm just like a pea
still perched in a pod,
but I know down inside
I'm the image of God....

Tom was asked by his classmates to read his collection of poems at the baccalaureate service.

Maureen had made peanut brittle and she passed it around. As we savored her treat, she told how she had made it, and what the toddler she was babysitting got into while she waited for the syrup to boil.

Fred, a tall, slender, neatly dressed senior was next. He had a large, thin book tucked under his arm that looked to be well-worn. He asked to sit at the top of the circle. As he brought the book from under his arm, he said, "I'm going to share with you my favorite book from childhood. It's called *The Velveteen Rabbit*." Fred's manner was serious and sincere. As he read the pages, he paused to pass around the pictures for all to see. When he finished reading, he said, "I find a lot of philosophy in this story all tied up in the question, 'What is *real*?' and the answer is, '*Real* isn't how you are made...it's a thing that happens to you. When a child loves you for a long, long time, not just to play with, but *really* loves you, then you become *real*.' That's the kind of love I'm looking for." There was a long pause of silence, and then one by one the students began to applaud and Fred smiled as he returned to his place.

The next day, Dan signaled to be the first to share. "For my final sharing, I want to tell you about my grandmother and the great impact that she has had on my life. I'm the middle child of seven children, and one of four boys. We are a very closely knit family, and proud of our ties to Ireland, the church, and each other. We were also very proud of and close to our grandmother who lived a block from our church. Every Sunday, after church, we would go to grandma's for breakfast. What a treat it was. She had been up since dawn, gone to early Mass, and had been cooking a full hour before our arrival. As we opened her door we were greeted with smells of good food wafting from her kitchen, and the sound of her singing a favorite Irish song. Grandma loved to sing as well as cook. With ten around her table, our knees were touching, but we didn't mind. Her food was so good, so plentiful, and the conversation never stopped.

"Also, it was very special for the child in the eighth grade who got to have lunch with Gram every day that school year. I could hardly wait until it was my turn. My older brothers would tell of their hot lunches and special treats. Often they would tell, too, how smart they thought she was. You could ask her anything. My mother said, 'She's wise.' Best of all though, she was a good listener. I can remember, when I was very young, hearing my parents talk about me, saying that I was hyperkinetic and how expensive the medicine would be. I remember being so worried about what it meant, and that we couldn't afford the expense. It was one of the things that I asked Grandma about. 'Don't worry yourself, Dan. That just means that you have more energy than other people. God gave you more energy, so that you can do more than others. Think of it that way, and you will do great things.'

"Grandma was the reason that I ran for student body president. I knew if I were elected, she'd be so proud. And she was. Then for the canned food drive for the poor, she set our goal at 15,000 cans, not 10,000, and we made it.

"But back to that eighth grade year. I not only had lunch with Gram, I sang with her as well. Her two favorite songs were 'How Great Thou Art' and 'Amazing Grace.' I used to wonder that neighbors didn't call, as our voices seemed to rise so high. One day she said to me, 'You have a very good voice, Danny. You are an Irish tenor. I don't know how it will be when you get older, but your voice is good now. I read in the church bulletin that they're having tryouts for the Boys' Choir. I'd like you to try out. There's talk that the choir will go on tour. That would be a good experience for you, in front of people and all.' I protested. 'No buts. Tryouts are tonight. I've already talked to your parents. If you make it, I'll pay your tour costs.' I hugged her extra hard that day. She patted my back soundly as we hugged, and said, 'You've got to get started using that extra energy.' Well, I made the Boys' Choir, and we went on tour. My grandma was so proud. We would practice after lunch, and I began to enjoy singing as much as she did. It was a great year.

"Just before this past Christmas, Grandma died. She went quickly, still at her home. As plans were being made for her funeral, my mother came to me and said, 'Dan, at the pause after communion for meditation, I want you to sing one of her favorite hymns.' I told her that I didn't think that I could. My voice would crack, I said, and I might cry. She assured me that I could do it. She said, 'Think of it as a tribute to Grandma.'"

Unnoticed until that moment was a tape recorder that Dan had switched on. With tears streaming down his cheeks, he allowed his classmates to share the beauty of his tenor voice reaching high in praise, as he sang:

> O Lord, my God, when I in awesome wonder
> Consider all the worlds Thy hands hath made;
> I see the stars, I hear the roaring thunder,
> Thy power throughout the universe displayed;
> Then sings my soul, my Savior God, to Thee;
> How great Thou art! How great Thou art!
> Then sings my soul, my Savior God, to Thee;
> How great Thou art! How great Thou art!

Objectives: For each of us to share something that is important to our life
To let others know us better

EXERCISE/JOURNAL SHEET

THE FINAL SHARING

Suggested categories:

1. Something I would like to share that tells about

    a. Who I am

    b. What is important to me

2. Something original I'd like to share

    a. Creative work I have done

    b. An interesting experience from my life

3. A talent

    a. Art

    b. Music: singing, playing an instrument

    c. Poetry, essay, short story

    d. Film

    e. Other

4. Something that I read and want to share

5. A quotation—as it pertains to my life, or as I have seen it expressed in someone else's life

6. Witness to my faith in God

7. My philosophy of life

8. Other

WRITE an outline of your final sharing. Include the who, what, and why.

TOPIC: _____ DATE: _____

BIBLIOGRAPHY

Alan Guttmacher Institute, The. *Sex and America's Teenagers*. New York. 1994. pp. 4, 29-30, 41, 72.

Bach, Richard. *Illusions: The Reluctant Messiah*. New York: Dell, 1979.

Bachelder, Louise. *On Friendship, A Selection*. Mount Vernon, NY: Peter Pauper Press, 1966.

Barth, Richard P. *Reducing the Risks: Building Skills to Prevent Pregnancy, STD and HIV*. Santa Cruz, Ca: ERT Associates, 1993. pp. 40, 164, 167-170.

Bode, Janet. *Kids Having Kids*. New York: Franklin Watts, 1980. pp. 193-194.

Britten, Benjamin. *War Requiem*. New York: Boosey and Hawkes, 1961.

Buscaglia, Leo. *Love*. New York: Fawcett Press, 1972. p. 131.

Feminization of Poverty Series, The. (Video). Part I: *No Way! Not Me!* VHS #113C 187. 104.29 minutes, 39 seconds. Toronto: The National Film Board of Canada. Ontario Production Centre, 1987.

Francis, Dorothy B. *Suicide, a Preventable Tragedy*. New York: Lodestar Books, 1989. p. 19.

Frankl, Victor E. *Man's Search for Meaning*. New York: Pocket Books, 1963. pp. 137, 104, 117.

Gardner, Sandra and Rosenberg, Gary. *Teenage Suicide*. New York: Julian Messner, 1990. pp 49, 55.

Gilbert, Sara. *Get Help, Solving the Problems in Your Life*. New York: Morrow Junior Books, 1989.

Glore, John. *Teenage Parents*. Vero Beach, CA: Rourke, 1990.

Grollman, Earl A. *Suicide: Prevention, Intervention, Postvention*. Boston: Beacon Press, 1988. pp. 68, 116.

Hart, Johnny. "B.C." Akron, OH: *Akron Beacon Journal*, November 20, 1988.

Hine, Stuart K. *How Great Thou Art*. Burbank, CA: Manna Music, 1955.

Inciardi, James. "Getting Busted for Drugs." pp. 63-83 in Beschner, George and Alfred Friedman, eds. *Teen Drug Use*. Lexington, MA: Lexington Books, 1986.

Joel, Billy. *James*. Turnstiles Album. New York: Columbia Records, 1976.

Johnston, Lynn. "Better or Worse." Akron, OH: *Akron Beacon Journal*, May 31, 1994.

Kennedy, Eugene C. *Crisis Counseling*. New York: Continuum, 1981. p 44.

———. *Loneliness and Everyday Problems*. New York: Image Books, 1983.

———. *The New Sexuality: Myths, Fables, Hang-ups*. New York: Doubleday, 1972. pp. 144, 138.

Klagsbrun, Francine. *Too Young to Die: Suicide and Youth*. Boston: Houghton Mifflin, 1976, p. 173.

Landers, Ann. "Teenage Girl Laments Allowing Boys to Have Sex." Akron, OH: *The Beacon Journal*, October 1, 1993.

Langone, John. *Dead End: A Book about Suicide*. Boston: Little, Brown and Company, 1986. pp. 112-113.

Lara, Adair. *Conspiracy of Kindness*. New York: *Glamour*, December 1991.

Laurence, Leslie, "Ignorance of Venereal Disease." Akron, OH: *The Beacon Journal*, March 3, 1994.

Mandino, Og. *The Greatest Miracle in the World*. New York: Lifetime Books 1975. pp. 104, 103.

Marx, Martin B, Thomas F. Garrity, and Frank R. Bowers. "The Influence of Recent Life Experience on the Health of College Freshmen." London: *Journal of Psychosomatic Research*, Vol. 19, pp. 87-98.

McCleary, Kathleen. "Sex, Morals and AIDS." New York: USA Weekend, December 29, 1991.

Morrison, Douglas and Christopher Witt. *From Loneliness to Love.* New York: Paulist Press, 1989. p. 48.

Muller, Robert. "The Power of Forgiveness." New York: Christopher News Notes, #347. July/August 1992.

National Household Survey on Drug Abuse. *When Drug Abuse Begins.* Rockville, MD: Substance Abuse and Mental Health Service Administration, 1991.

National Institute of Mental Health. *Adolescence and Depression.* Rockville, MD: Substance Abuse and Mental Health Service Administration, 1981.

Peck, M. Scott. *The Road Less Traveled.* New York: A Touchstone Book. Simon & Schuster, 1978. p. 82.

Powell, John. *Free to Be Me.* Niles, IL: Argus Communications, 1978. pp. 12, 6.

Richo, David. *How to Be an Adult.* New York: Paulist Press, 1991. pp. 52, 49, 111, 110.

Safran, Claire. "Let's Get Wasted." New York: *Ladies Home Journal,* December 1991.

Sheehan, Sharon A. "Another Kind of Sex Education." New York: *Newsweek,* July 13, 1992.

Townsend, Mary C. *Psychiatric Mental Health Nursing: Concepts of Care.* Philadelphia: F. A. Davis, 1993.

Webster's New World Dictionary, Student Edition. New York: Simon & Schuster, 1983.

Williams, Margery. *The Velveteen Rabbit.* New York: Alfred A. Knopf, 1983. p. 12.

Wymelenberg, Suzanne. *Science and Babies (Private Decision. Public Dilemma).* Washington, DC: National Academy Press, 1990.